THE LIVES AND WORKS OF
THE PRE-RAPHAELITES

THE LIVES AND WORKS OF
THE PRE-RAPHAELITES

AN ILLUSTRATED EXPLORATION OF THE PRE-RAPHAELITE BROTHERHOOD, THEIR
LIVES AND CONTEXTS, WITH A GALLERY OF 290 OF THEIR GREATEST PAINTINGS

MICHAEL ROBINSON

HERMES
HOUSE

This edition is published by Hermes House, an imprint of Anness Publishing Ltd, Blaby Road, Wigston, Leicestershire LE18 4SE; info@anness.com

www.hermeshouse.com; www.annesspublishing.com

Anness Publishing has a new picture agency outlet for images for publishing, promotions or advertising. Please visit our website www.practicalpictures.com for more information.

ETHICAL TRADING POLICY:

At Anness Publishing we believe that business should be conducted in an ethical and ecologically sustainable way, with respect for the environment and a proper regard to the replacement of the natural resources we employ.

As a publisher, we use a lot of wood pulp in high-quality paper for printing, and that wood commonly comes from spruce trees. We are therefore currently growing more than 750,000 trees in three Scottish forest plantations: Berrymoss (130 hectares/ 320 acres), West Touxhill (125 hectares/ 305 acres) and Deveron Forest (75 hectares/185 acres). The forests we manage contain more than 3.5 times the number of trees employed each year in making paper for the books we manufacture.

Because of this ongoing ecological investment programme, you, as our customer, can have the pleasure and reassurance of knowing that a tree is being cultivated on your behalf to naturally replace the materials used to make the book you are holding.

Our forestry programme is run in accordance with the UK Woodland Assurance Scheme (UKWAS) and will be certified by the internationally recognized Forest Stewardship Council (FSC). The FSC is a non-government organization dedicated to promoting responsible management of the world's forests. Certification ensures forests are managed in an environmentally sustainable and socially responsible way. For further information about this scheme, go to www.annesspublishing.com/trees

Publisher: Joanna Lorenz
Project Editor: Daniel Hurst
Designer: Sarah Rock
Production Controller: Christine Ni

PUBLISHER'S NOTE

Although the advice and information in this book are believed to be accurate and true at the time of going to press, neither the authors nor the publisher can accept any legal responsibility or liability for any errors or omissions that may have been made, nor for any inaccuracies.

PICTURES: p1 JE Millais, *The Proscribed Royalist, 1651*, 1852–3, p2 John Brett, *The Hedger*, 1860, p3 JW Waterhouse, *The Lady of Shalott,* 1884

CONTENTS

Introduction	6
THE PRE-RAPHAELITES, THEIR LIVES AND TIMES	**8**
JOHN EVERETT MILLAIS	10
DANTE GABRIEL ROSSETTI	30
WILLIAM HOLMAN HUNT	52
ARTISTS ASSOCIATED WITH THE MOVEMENT	74
THE GALLERY	**100**
A NEW AESTHETIC 1847–1854	102
INTO THE MAINSTREAM 1855–1860	124
THE SECOND WAVE OF PRE-RAPHAELITISM 1861–1870	160
AESTHETIC PRE-RAPHAELITISM 1870–1880	200
THE FINAL YEARS, AFTER 1890	236
Index	254

INTRODUCTION

The Pre-Raphaelite archetype may conjure up visions of tragic, flame-haired women posing as famous literary heroines, but the Brotherhood's true impetus was rooted in a desire to rebel against traditional aesthetic conventions and to accurately portray nature in all her glory.

After the Napoleonic Wars of 1799–1881, Great Britain enjoyed a relatively peaceful period. Queen Victoria (1819–1901) was crowned in 1838 and was a welcome change from her rather decadent and aloof Hanoverian predecessors. Her marriage to Prince Albert (1819–61) and the birth of their first child in 1840 ensured the stability and continuation of the monarchy, something also missing from the reigns of the previous two monarchs. Nevertheless a revolution was to take place in Britain, the undermining of traditional painting at the most august of artistic institutions, the Royal Academy. In 1843 John Ruskin (1819–1900) published his book *Modern Painters*, a defence of the non-academic experiments of the artist JMW Turner (1775–1851), that is also a didactic treatise urging artists to

document nature more faithfully. Like many young artists of their generation, the Pre-Raphaelites were to become devotees of Ruskin, disillusioned with the Academy Schools' manner of teaching. Ruskin aspired to establish "the foundations of a school of art nobler than the world has seen for three hundred years".

A BROTHERHOOD

In the autumn of 1848, a group of like-minded artists, John Everett Millais (1829–96), William Holman Hunt (1827–1910), and Dante Gabriel Rossetti (1828–82), met in London to discuss the rather lax style of traditional academic painting espoused by the Academy Schools, a style that began in the period following the High Renaissance painter Raphael (Raffaello Sanzio: 1483–1520). They blamed such

laxity in Britain on the advocate of this approach, the first president of the Academy, Sir Joshua Reynolds (1723–92), referred to by them later as 'Sir Sloshua'. In its place they wanted a lighter tone to the work that would dazzle in its freshness. This was an agenda for changing the face of British painting forever. They proposed a Brotherhood that would infiltrate the Academy and change it from within. There was a certain naivety in their ambitions, providing a number of 'heroes', both real and legendary, that could appear in, or inspire, their works. They included such diverse figures as Shakespeare, Dante, Jesus, Chaucer, Keats and King Arthur. Another four members were recruited to the Brotherhood: William Michael Rossetti (1829–1919), a poet and brother of Dante; Frederic George Stephens

Above: Joshua Reynolds, Self Portrait Wearing Glasses, *oil on panel, 1788.*

Above: William Hogarth, Falstaff Examining his Recruits, *from* Henry IV *by Shakespeare, oil on canvas, 1730.*

THE PRE-RAPHAELITES, THEIR LIVES AND TIMES

Formed in 1848, the Pre-Raphaelites were, at their core, a seven-member Brotherhood. However, the scope and influence of the Pre-Raphaelite ethos attracted many artists into the group's circle, and Pre-Raphaelitism transcends just the members of the Brotherhood. The following chapters examine the lives and works of key members of the group, including John Everett Millais, Dante Gabriel Rossetti and William Holman Hunt, but also look closely at the group's patrons and contemporaries, such as John Ruskin, Willam Morris, Ford Madox Brown and Edward Burne-Jones, among others, who did almost as much to further the influence and appreciation of the Pre-Raphaelite style as any of the 'official' members.

Left: DG Rossetti, Lady Lilith, *oil on canvas, 1864–8, Delaware Art Museum, USA, 98 x 85cm (39¼ x 34in).*

JOHN EVERETT MILLAIS

Millais was the young protégé of both the Royal Academy Schools and later, of his mentor John Ruskin. Having received his artistic training at the Academy Schools, the young Millais was to upset this august body in 1849 and 1850 by exhibiting works that contravened the accepted rules of Academic painting. He was also to alienate Ruskin by marrying his former wife. However, by the late 1850s he had returned to traditional subject matter, especially portraiture, and became a full member of the Academy, later becoming its president and rubbing shoulders with the élite of the art world. In later life he become a baronet, the first artist to do so since Godfrey Kneller in the 17th century, and the very first to be awarded a hereditary title. Millais was also celebrated in France, and established his reputation at two successive World's Fairs.

Above: JP Mayall, John Everett Millais, *photograph, 1884.*
Left: JE Millais, The Order of Release, *watercolour, c.1863.*

EARLY YEARS

Born to wealthy parents, John Everett Millais was encouraged and promoted in his artistic endeavours from an early age. His talent for drawing led to him enrolling in the Royal Academy at the age of 11, nurturing his talents whilst exposing him to the artistic styles he would eventually rebel against.

John Everett Millais was born in Southampton, England, on the 8th June 1829 into a prosperous family with independent financial means. He was the third child of John William Millais (1800–70), from Jersey, and Mary Emily Evamy (1789–1864), from Southampton; both their families were well-to-do. Between 1831 and 1834, the family lived in Jersey, before relocating to Dinan in Brittany until 1837.

FORMATIVE YEARS

As a young boy, John showed a natural talent for drawing, and in particular for portraiture. Initially, he was taught by Edward Henry Wehnert (1813–1868),

an accomplished Anglo-German genre artist, living in Jersey at the time. Millais' parents both recognized and wished to nurture their son's talents, and decided to move to London in 1838 so that the young boy could study at the private art school of Henry Sass (1788–1844). Sass was a well-respected artist who taught several artists to draw in their early careers, including two future presidents of the Royal Academy. Millais' talent was, however, beyond the scope of Sass and, two years later, with Sass's support, he enrolled in the Royal Academy Schools, its youngest ever pupil at just 11 years of age.

A CONSERVATIVE REBEL

In 1843, Millais' friend William Holman Hunt was accepted as a probationer at the Royal Academy Schools. Millais had already met Hunt, who was to become a lifelong friend, when the two had been sketching in the British Museum a few months before. Like many young artists of their generation, Millais and Hunt rebelled against the formulaic approach to teaching painting and drawing of the Academy Schools, based largely on the *Discourses* of Sir Joshua

Below: Richard Banks Harraden, Drawing in Life Class at the Royal Academy, *engraving, date unknown.*

Below right: *JE Millais,* Pizarro Seizing the Inca of Peru, *oil on canvas, 1846.*

THE ROYAL ACADEMY

At the time of Millais' enrolment, the president of the Royal Academy was Martin Archer Shee (1769–1850), a portraitist who had succeeded Sir Thomas Lawrence (1769–1830) as president, in 1830. This was the ideal time for an artist such as Millais, essentially a portraitist, to come to the fore. His mother was aware of this and arranged for her son to be seen by Shee. In 1843, Millais won the Academy's silver medal for his *Drawing from the Antique* in 1843. His painting of *Pizarro Seizing the Inca of Peru* was his first shown at the Royal Academy exhibition of 1846, which he followed up by the more impressive *The Tribe of Benjamin Seizing the Daughters of Shiloh*, which won the gold medal in 1847. *Pizarro* also won the gold medal when it was shown at the Society of Arts in 1847.

Reynolds. They were also both inspired by John Ruskin's *Modern Painters*, which sought to undermine this tradition by suggesting that artists be more faithful in documenting nature in their work. All students of the Royal Academy Schools were entitled to study there for ten years, but both Millais and Hunt did not complete their respective courses, preferring instead to carve out a new and more radical path.

TOWARD 1848

Millais' parents took a lease on a house at 83 Gower St, in London, between 1844 and 1854, providing their son with a ground floor studio. It was here that he painted his first self-portrait in 1847, his boyish looks belying his mature mastery of the oil medium. At this time he was still a student at the Academy and was affectionately known as 'The Child' due to his boyish appearance.

FIRST STEPS

Having established himself at the Royal Academy Schools, Millais began, with his contemporaries, to consider how he might challenge modern aesthetics to develop as an artist. This discontent with the artistic convention soon led to the formation of the Pre-Raphaelite Brotherhood.

Millais was a member of the so-called Cyclographic Society in 1848, to which he and other artists brought their sketches for mutual criticism at their monthly meetings. This was an important precursor to what followed, the formation of the Pre-Raphaelite Brotherhood (PRB), since all but Dante Gabriel Rossetti belonged to the society.

THE FIRST MEETING

In the early autumn of 1848, Millais effectively presided over the inaugural meeting of the group at his home in Gower Street. The aim was to discuss how they might develop as artists, while adhering to Ruskin's tenets and avoiding

Below left: JE Millais, James Wyatt and his Granddaughter, *1848, watercolour.*

the inauthentic rigours of their Academy training. During the rest of that year and into the winter of 1849, the group met to decide how best to undermine the establishment and to present a united front at the forthcoming Academy exhibition. It was decided that they append the letters 'PRB' to the signature of each artist on their respective paintings.

ISABELLA

Millais' first submission to the Royal Academy after the formation of the PRB was *Isabella,* or *Lorenzo and Isabella.* The image links a revival of medievalism with 19th-century literary Romanticism. The subject of the picture is from the Florentine writer Giovanni Boccaccio's *Decameron* of 1353, a collection of tales which in turn influenced the English writer Geoffrey Chaucer, from whom other Pre-Raphaelite artists drew inspiration. Boccaccio's tale was retold by the English 19th-century poet John Keats, and concerns the tragic love story of Isabella, a wealthy merchant's daughter who has fallen in love with Lorenzo, a lowly apprentice of her brothers, who are showing their annoyance and contempt of the union in this painting. The style is based on the *Quattrocento* (early 15th-century) Florentine paintings, predating the later High Renaissance concerns of perspective and illusion, and concentrating on the colour and decorative qualities of the image. Millais' costumes are faithful to the *Quattrocento* but he has used recognizable contemporary figures as his sitters; for example, his father is shown in the centre wiping his mouth on a napkin. The picture was sold, and Millais wrote to Rossetti that 'the success of the PRB is now *quite certain*'.

CRITICISM OF MILLAIS

Criticism of *Isabella* was generally favourable, with most critics recognizing the influence of the

Left: JE Millais, Lorenzo and Isabella, *watercolour, c.1848.*

EARLY PORTRAITS

From an early age Millais was able to capture a good likeness in his portraits, a talent that he turned to his financial advantage. Millais had become acquainted with an art dealer in Oxford, James Wyatt (1774–1853), who was to become a patron of the PRB artists. In 1848, Wyatt asked Millais to paint a portrait of himself with his four-year-old granddaughter. This is one of several portraits of the Wyatt family that the artist painted around this time. These portraits follow the ideals of the PRB in the use of bright colour on a light background, eschewing the *chiaroscuro* effects used in contemporary Academic painting.

Florentine school. Although Millais had appended the letters PRB to his signature, most critics failed to notice. However, word soon circulated as to the letters' meaning, creating a furore in the art establishment. Critics were angry with the presumptuous secret society for its attempt to undermine

Academic traditions and values. The issue came to a head the next year with the publication of *The Germ*, a propagandist journal explaining the artistic views of the group.

Right: JE Millais, Self-portrait, *1847, oil on canvas.*

Below: JE Millais, Study for the Head of Ferdinand, *1849, graphite on paper.*

THE FIRST SCANDAL

After their formation, the Brotherhood believed it was important for them to establish and promote their agenda, leading them to publish a journal asserting their views and intentions. This, along with their art, began to draw the sometimes critical attention of many prominent public figures.

Toward the end of 1849, Rossetti and the writers in the PRB group first mooted the idea of a journal, one that was essentially a manifesto of the group's aims. The publication was named *The Germ*, and served to widen public knowledge of the group's existence and intentions.

THE GERM

The first edition was published in January 1850. Although the journal was short-lived and a financial failure, it was the first time that a group of avowedly avant-garde artists had published their polemic. Furthermore, it encouraged other artists and writers to submit poems and articles for consideration. One such article was by the sculptor John Lucas Tupper, who wrote: '… (the artist's) best and most original ideas are derived from his own time … why transfer them to distant periods and make them not of things today?' This call for artists to seek modern subjects for modern paintings is contemporary to a similar call by the poet Charles Baudelaire (1821–67) in Paris. Some of the Pre-Raphaelite artists responded by depicting contemporary social issues. Millais, however, decided to give a contemporary feel to a traditional religious narrative.

CHRIST IN THE HOUSE OF HIS PARENTS

Like most aspiring artists, and particularly those studying at the Academy Schools, Millais would have been familiar with several traditional High Renaissance paintings at the National Gallery, including Correggio's *Madonna of the Basket*, acquired in 1825, which depicts Mary dressing the infant Jesus. She appears to have made

Right: WP Frith, Portrait of Charles Dickens, *oil on canvas, 1859.*

his blue coat, as alluded to by the basket containing wool next to her, and by the title of the painting. In other Renaissance paintings, Mary is traditionally shown at a spinning wheel. In the background of Correggio's picture, Joseph is working as a carpenter in something of an Arcadian landscape. These images help to explain the furore caused by Millais' picture *Christ in the House of His Parents* (also known as *The Carpenter' Shop*); his

Right: JE Millais, Head of Mariana (study), *oil on panel, 1851.*

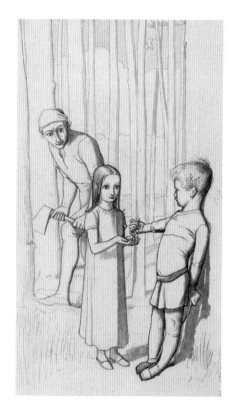

Above: JE Millais Study for 'The Woodman's Daughter', *pen and ink, 1849.*

contemporary carpentry shop. Mary Hodgkinson, the artist's sister-in-law and model for *Isabella*, modelled for Christ's mother, while Joseph was modelled by a London grocer, so that Millais could establish the physique of a working man. The biggest controversy was over the extent of the realism used in the picture, such as the dirty toenails and red working hands of St Anne in the background, which were seen by many as blasphemous.

CHARLES DICKENS

Among the many vociferous voices against Millais' picture, exhibited at the Royal Academy in 1850, was the prominent writer and novelist Charles Dickens (1812–70). It is worth recalling his words in detail, describing the portrayal of Jesus as a 'hideous, wry-necked, blubbering red-haired boy in a nightgown, who appears to have received a poke playing in a gutter, and to be holding it up for the contemplation of a kneeling woman, so horrible in her ugliness that she would stand out from the rest of the company as a monster in the vilest cabaret in France or the lowest

Above: FX Winterhalter, Portrait of Queen Victoria, *oil on canvas, 1842.*

gin-shop in London'. Dickens' article, published in the magazine *Household Words*, was one of many written by people whose sensibilities had been outraged, but coming from such a popular and esteemed writer made it particularly poignant, although it had the desired effect for the Brotherhood, who had deliberately set out to upset the establishment. By this time, the true meaning of the PRB monogram was well known, which further incensed many people because these were the young men who had dared to challenge Academic tradition and rigour.

QUEEN VICTORIA

The Queen, the figurehead for tradition and moral values at the time, became interested in the furore and arranged to have *Christ in the House of His Parents* sent to Buckingham Palace, with Millais writing to Holman Hunt that he hoped it would not 'have any bad effect on her mind'. Despite the adverse publicity, the picture was sold to the art dealer Henry Farrar for £300 (equivalent today to about £25,000), who then sold it on to Thomas Plint (1823–61), one of the new Pre-Raphaelite collectors.

RUSKIN'S INTERVENTION

After receiving public criticism and backlash from the wider artistic community, it was important for the Pre-Raphaelites to gain some support for their cause. This came in the form of John Ruskin, a respected art critic, who applauded the group's move toward a more naturalistic artistic aesthetic.

The Pre-Raphaelites had suffered written abuse at the hands of several writers in 1850, and it was John Ruskin who defended them after Millais' patron Thomas Combe (1796–1872) had asked the critic to intervene on their behalf.

JOHN RUSKIN

In many ways, John Ruskin epitomized the Victorian gentleman in terms of education, dress, propriety and religious values. However, his unorthodox approach to the arts was anathema to the establishment, eschewing the conventions of painting in favour of embracing the natural world. He first came to prominence at the tender age

Above: JE Millais, Ophelia, *watercolour, 1865.*

Right: JE Millais, Elizabeth Siddall study for Ophelia, *pencil, 1852.*

of 17, when defending the painter JMW Turner against vitriolic attacks he had undergone from members of the establishment. Ruskin was also responsible for promulgating Gothic

architecture in two of his most famous essays, *The Seven Lamps of Architecture* (1849) and *The Stones of Venice* (1851–3), advocating a 'truth to materials'.

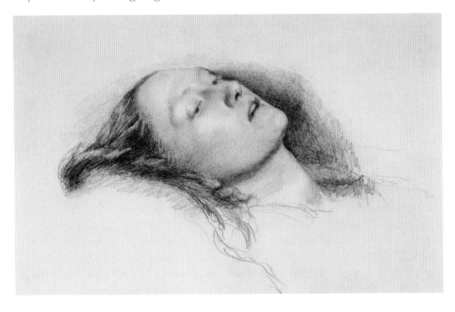

Despite not having even made the acquaintance of any of the Brotherhood, Ruskin wrote to *The Times* at Thomas Combe's request, applauding their use of naturalism and suggesting that they had the potential to create a more 'honest art' than had been seen in 300 years.

Following this letter to *The Times*, Millais wrote to Ruskin thanking him for defending their position. Ruskin's letter had been a genuine critique of the work and was not entirely laudatory, but it was enough to put an end to the vitriolic abuse of other critics. On receiving Millais' letter, Ruskin went to Gower St with his young wife Effie and took the artist back to their house in Camberwell, South London, where he remained for a week as a guest.

WORKING WITH HOLMAN HUNT

Ruskin also invited Holman Hunt to stay at his home with Millais, but he was unavailable. When Millais returned from the Ruskins', he was full of enthusiasm for the future of the Brotherhood, which he communicated to Holman Hunt. The two Brothers agreed to set up a studio together outside central London, and took lodgings at Surbiton Hill in Surrey. Their stay was short before moving to the nearby Worcester Park Farm in Cheam, where Charles Collins (1828–73) joined them. It was at this location that several major paintings were

Below: William Downey, Portrait of John Ruskin, *photograph, 1863.*

devised and executed, using the surrounding countryside as reference for the backgrounds. Millais painted the backgrounds to *The Huguenot* and *Ophelia* – possibly his most famous picture. All the landscape detail for *Ophelia* was executed at the Hogsmill River. This picture led to a change in Millais' reputation. Such detailed depiction of foliage would certainly follow Ruskin's dictum that the artist 'go to nature in all singleness of heart, rejecting nothing and selecting nothing'. However, it was other critics who praised this picture; and its inclusion at the Exposition Universelle in Paris, in 1855, cemented his international reputation.

Below: JE Millais, Portrait of Holman Hunt, *watercolour, 1854.*

ASSOCIATE OF THE ACADEMY

Despite his opposition of the conventions of his artistic training, Millais still craved the approval of the establishment. Under Ruskin's tutelage he had learned to curb his radical approach while maintaining his artistic ideals; this led to greater recognition and eventual election to the Royal Academy.

Millais was disappointed at not being elected an Associate of the Royal Academy in November 1852. An opening had arisen in the academy with the death of JMW Turner the previous December. At the age of 23 Millais was too young by a year and instead the vacancy was taken by the genre painter Frederick Goodall (1822–1904).

THE ROYAL ACADEMY

Despite railing against the traditions of the Royal Academy as part of the Brotherhood, Millais still craved their approval. On hearing the news of his rejection at this election in 1852, Millais

threatened never to exhibit again at the Royal Academy. The following year, however, Millais was elected an Associate, thanks in no small part to both John and Effie Ruskin, and the Academy exhibition of 1853 marked a watershed in the fortunes of the Pre-Raphaelite Brothers, who all enjoyed success. Michael William Rossetti remarked: 'We have emerged from reckless abuse to a position of high recognition.'

THE RUSKINS

John Ruskin's defence of the Pre-Raphaelites, and his adoption of Millais as his protégé, had persuaded the artist

to be less radical in his approach to painting without compromising his artistic integrity. His painting of *A Huguenot on St Bartholomew's Day* (1851–2) was an attempt to achieve this. The background was completed first, while Millais was working with Holman Hunt, and demonstrates his fidelity to nature. The couple, painted in later, show an endearing tenderness and participate in a narrative acceptable to the establishment of the mid-19th century, and thus to the Academy. In a very short space of time, Millais had managed to adopt a style of painting acceptable to the establishment that he had previously rejected and, with Ruskin's help and guidance, had established a new era in British painting. This change of style was enhanced by his use of Effie Ruskin (1828–97) as his model. Effie posed for *The Order of Release*, completed in 1853, in which her expression is one of mixed emotions untypical of the time. Parts of the narrative are ambiguous because of this expression, and this may reflect the intimacy that was developing between the artist and his model.

SCOTLAND

In the summer of 1853, following the exhibition success of *The Order of Release* at the Royal Academy, Millais left London with his brother William Henry (1828–99) and a group of others, including John and Effie Ruskin, visiting Glenfinlas in the Highlands of Scotland to spend time painting and fishing. It is unclear when the topic of a portrait of Ruskin by Millais was first mooted, but a formal portrait of the critic was begun in late July. It was not completed however until late 1854. The weather in that first summer was unfavourable for outdoor painting, and

Left: After JE Millais, Portrait of Ruskin, *photogravure, date unknown.*

Above: WH Millais, Glenfinlas with Millais Fishing, *oil on panel, 1853.*

Millais was unable to complete the portrait. He returned, this time without the Ruskins, to paint the background of the picture in 1854. Ruskin also visited Millais' London studio in the same year so that he could complete the portrait.

EFFIE

A native Scot, Effie was unhappy with her older husband at the time of the trip to Glenfinlas, and fell in love with Millais, who was of a similar age. This relationship, and the breakdown of her marriage to Ruskin, scandalized Victorian society and caused great pain to the three protagonists in the affair. However, both Ruskin and Millais remained professional and completed the portrait. Millais had also fallen in love with Scotland, returning there many times during his life.

Above: After JE Millais, Self-portrait, *lithograph, date unknown.*

Above: JE Millais, Turner on Varnishing Day, *pen and ink, 1851.*

A SECOND SCANDAL

The turbulent backdrop of the Crimean War provided Millais with new inspiration for his work. However, the annulment of the Ruskin's marriage and the part Millais supposedly played in its breakdown caused public outrage, temporarily impeding his rise to fame.

THE CRIMEAN WAR

1854 was a turbulent year for Millais, the Ruskins and Britain in general. In March, Great Britain, France and the Ottomans declared war on the Russian Empire over disagreements concerning the Holy Land. The conflict, which lasted until 1856, claimed the lives of 20,000 British soldiers, most of whom died from diseases contracted in the Crimean peninsula. It was these losses and the appalling lack of sanitary hospital care for the wounded that led to radical changes in the nursing regime by Florence Nightingale (1820–1910). Although Millais did not paint scenes from the conflict itself, many of his works, such as *A Huguenot on St Bartholomew's Day* and *The Proscribed Royalist*, explore the theme of the stoic woman and the vulnerable man. At the end of the conflict, Millais painted one of his most famous pictures, an exemplar of this subject, *Peace Concluded*. His work from this period found favour at the Academy exhibitions and helped to elevate his status as an artist. Although his ties to the Brotherhood were not formally severed, Millais seemed from this point to have set a distance between himself and his colleagues, although he continued to embrace aspects of the Pre-Raphaelite style.

SCANDAL

Just as Millais' reputation as an artist was being elevated, he was embroiled in a scandal about the irretrievable breakdown of the Ruskins' marriage. It transpired later that the marriage was annulled on the grounds of non-consummation, as confirmed by Ruskin during the annulment proceedings. In April 1854, Effie left the marital home, and in July the court formally ended the marriage. The annulment appeared not to harm Ruskin's career as a writerb. Shortly after these events he changed from art criticism to social politics.

MOVING HOME AND STUDIO

During 1854, Millais moved his studio twice and led a somewhat peripatetic lifestyle, for both pragmatic and emotional reasons. In the early summer, the Millais family moved from Gower St to Kingston upon Thames, where the artist had a studio above a stable block. He also spent several weeks in Scotland finishing the Ruskin portrait, and, on his return journey, stayed with friends in Derbyshire. New paintings, most

Above: JE Millais, Accepted, *pen and sepia ink, 1853.*

notably *The Blind Girl*, were begun while he was staying in Winchelsea in Sussex late that summer. Millais particularly enjoyed the medieval atmosphere of this ancient port, and, true to Ruskinian ideals, painted the background from nature. In October of that year, the artist took a studio in London's West End, which he retained until 1859.

Right: JE Millais, A Study of Effie Gray, pen and ink, date unknown.

Far right: JE Millais, An Actor, pencil, date unknown.

ALFRED, LORD TENNYSON

Millais had continued to use themes and characters from Alfred, Lord Tennyson's poems since painting *Mariana* in 1851. When the picture was first exhibited at the Academy, lines from the poem of the same name accompanied it. However, Millais in fact based the painting on Tennyson's source, the character in Shakespeare's *Measure for Measure*. It is an evocation of Mariana's longing to be rescued from a life of loneliness and sexual frustration. Having left Cambridge University without a degree, Tennyson came to prominence in the 1830s with his epic poem *The Lady of Shalott*, which inspired several of the Pre-Raphaelite artists who were also interested in Arthurian legends. In 1850, at the time the Pre-Raphaelite enterprise was burgeoning, Tennyson was made Poet Laureate, meaning he was effectively in charge of poetry for formal state occasions. One such occasion was the charge of the light brigade during the Crimean War, a heroic cavalry charge that resulted in the loss of many soldiers; it was immortalized by Tennyson in his poem of 1854. Millais' interest in Tennyson's poetry brought him into contact with the poet, with whom he stayed in the autumn of that year. It was a lasting friendship that resulted in Millais, among others, illustrating the Edward Moxon edition of Tennyson's poems published in 1857, and culminated in a portrait of the artist in 1881.

Right: JE Millais, Portrait of Alfred, Lord Tennyson, oil on canvas, 1881.

MARRIAGE TO EFFIE

The year after the Ruskin marriage was annulled, Millais married Effie. The marriage was a happy one, but the controversial circumstances surrounding their romance led to Effie being ostracized by society. The couple moved to Scotland to escape the public scrutiny and focus on Millais' work.

The furore surrounding the breakdown of John and Effie Ruskin's marriage had brought Millais further under public scrutiny – but for personal, rather than professional, reasons. As a result, it was important for the artist to remind the world of his artistic skill and distance himself from scandal.

A ROW AT THE ACADEMY

At the Royal Academy exhibition of 1855, Millais' *The Rescue* was poorly hung, with the artist causing a scene when he abused some of the officials. Although the work was critically well received and sold for £580 (equivalent today to about £40,000), the star of the exhibition that year was Leighton's *Cimabue's Madonna*, which was sold to Queen Victoria for a similar sum. This was Leighton's first major work shown at the Royal Academy, and to sell it to the monarch both sealed his reputation and facilitated his rise to President of the Academy in the election of 1878.

EFFIE

Despite the scandal of the previous year, Ruskin continued to support Millais critically, although his enthusiasm for his protégé had understandably waned. In response to *The Rescue*,

Above: *JE Millais,* A Wife, *watercolour, date unknown.*

Ruskin remarked: 'It is the only great picture this year and it is very great.' Following the Academy exhibition, Millais married Effie, and after a month's

Above: *French School,* Palais d'Industrie, *engraving, c.1855.*

THE GARRICK CLUB

Originally established in 1831 as a theatrical club named in homage to the 18th-century actor David Garrick, by the mid 19th-century the Garrick was an exclusive club for established writers and painters such as Charles Dickens and Millais. Perhaps in response to writers on contemporary issues such as Dickens, Millais painted the first of his genre subjects in 1855. *The Rescue* depicts a brave fireman rescuing children from a burning building, a scene that the artist himself had witnessed, although Dickens had discussed the motif with him as well. The Garrick has continued as an exclusive male-only club mainly for creative people.

honeymoon they moved in to Annat Lodge in Perth, Scotland, near her family's home. Effie was instrumental in designing many of the costumes worn by her and other models for her husband's pictures. The garden at Annat Lodge was used for the genre picture *Autumn Leaves*, which features Effie's two younger sisters, Alice and Sophie. In the background is the spire of the ancient church of St John. The picture is another departure for Millais: instead of a clear narrative, he is beginning to seek the ideal in beauty, suggesting that it can be found in the face of an eight-year-old girl 'before humanity is subject to such change'. The setting for the picture was inspired by Millais' visit to Tennyson at Farringford the previous year, when he helped sweep up and burn dead leaves in the poet's garden.

Below: G Fletcher, The Coffee Room at the Garrick Club, *watercolour, 1964.*

PARIS

Between May and November 1855, three of Millais' paintings were shown at the Exposition Universelle: *The Order of Release, Ophelia* and *The Return of the Dove to the Ark.* Millais had selected works from his earlier period, suggesting he was uncertain about the style he was developing by 1855.

The Exposition Universelle of 1855 was the first of its kind in Paris, and attempted to surpass the success of the Great Exhibition of 1851 in London. Certainly the art shown was superior to that found in England at the time, and paved the way for Paris's dominance as the artistic capital of Europe. The fact that Millais' paintings were included is an indication of his stature as an artist at this time.

Right: JE Millais, Portrait of Effie Ruskin, *watercolour, 1853.*

FINANCIAL SUCCESS

The mid-late 1850s were a lucrative and happy time for Millais; he received record sums for his paintings and the first of his eight children was born. Millais' financial gains were compounded by the fact he allowed prints of his works to be made, and also through his prolific work as an illustrator.

Millais was a commercially minded artist, and his willingness to exploit his art for financial gain meant that he was in monetary terms, the most successful of all the Pre-Raphaelite artists. Reproduction prints of his work were hugely popular and very lucrative.

FINANCIAL SUCCESS

The years 1856 and 1857 were the most successful period in Millais' career to date. In 1856 he earned over £2000 from the sale of three paintings at the Royal Academy. His financial triumph was also due in part to the success of

his images as reproductions, beginning with *A Huguenot*, published in 1856 by the London dealer David Thomas White. It was at this time that Millais' success was noticed by Ernest Gambart (1814–1902), the legendary print-seller.

Gambart purchased *The Blind Girl* in April 1856 for the sum of 400 guineas, selling it on the following year at a profit. By 1860 he was offering Joseph Arden 2,000 guineas for the picture *The Rescue* and its copyright, originally purchased in 1855 for £580. Gambart also purchased *The Black Brunswicker* in 1860 for the sum of 1,000 guineas, (about £75,000 today). Millais also made watercolour copies of this painting for the dealer, but it was the reproduction of the original image that made it so successful. Gambart made

Above: Charles Dodgson, Millais with his Wife and Daughters, *photograph, 1865.*

Left: JE Millais, A Huguenot, *pen, ink and gouache, 1852.*

vast sums of money from reproductions; his shrewd business sense was attuned to the Victorian penchant for sentimental, nostalgic and emotional images that often bordered on the saccharine.

Above: Edward Radclyffe, The Royal Academy, a Private View, *engraving, 1841.*

Below: JE Millais, Locksley Hall, an Illustration for the Moxon Tennyson, *wood engraving, 1857.*

ILLUSTRATION

The literary influences on Pre-Raphaelite paintings made the artists ideal book illustrators. Millais responded well to this demand, creating a series of 18 drawings for the 'Moxon Tennyson'. Millais understood the techniques well, producing one of the finest examples of the genre with *The Eve of St Agnes*. Millais was the most prolific of the Pre-Raphaelite illustrators, and also produced many one-offs for *The Illustrated London News*, *The Cornhill* and other popular magazines.

CHILDREN

On 30 May 1856, the first of Millais' and Effie's eight children, Everett Millais (1856–97), was born. Everett features in a number of paintings by Millais, most notably *The Boyhood of Raleigh* (1870), which also featured his second son, George. In 1868 Millais painted *Sisters*, a portrait of three of his daughters, in a style that came to be known as Aestheticism. The Aesthetic Movement aimed for a simpler art devoid of narrative having no political or social agenda, an 'art for art's sake'.

MILLAIS' LATTER YEARS

During the late 1850s, Millais received lukewarm reviews for several of his paintings. This crisis of confidence led to a move away from Pre-Raphaelite ideals, toward a more populist aesthetic style that allowed him to focus on illustration and society-portrait painting to support his growing family.

During the final years of his career, Millais began to move even further away from the Pre-Raphaelite ideals that he had once so fervently propagated. This shift in style led to critical backlash and accusations that Millais had compromised his artistic ideals for wealth and popularity.

HIATUS
Although financially successful, Millais was still subject to criticism, even from his previous champion, Ruskin. When the artist submitted the painting *A Dream of the Past: Sir Isumbras at the Ford* to the Academy in 1857, Ruskin accused the work of displaying the 'pathetic fallacy' (the attribution of human qualities to inanimate natural objects), saying it lacked 'truth to nature' and required too much input from the viewer's imagination. This, however, is what the artist intended as he moved even further away from Pre-Raphaelitism. The painting *Autumn Leaves* was the first sign of this shift toward a more melancholic mood in his work, embracing emotions such as pathos rather than rendering the Ruskinian ideals he had followed in his early career. Millais was also dealing with the transience of life in *Vale of Rest* as well as *Sir Isumbras at the Ford* and *Autumn Leaves*. These paintings failed to impress an indifferent public at the 1859 Academy exhibition, and it was not until the following year, when *The Black Brunswicker* was shown, that confidence was restored. Ernest Gambart, Millais' new champion, purchased the painting for 1,000 guineas.

THE 1860S AND 1870S
Following the crisis in public confidence, Millais relied more on illustration work than paintings to provide an income for his growing family. However, he continued to explore a new mode of painting, seeking to develop his own

Above: JE Millais, The Black Brunswicker, *engraving, 1863.*

Left: JE Millais, Cherry Ripe, *oil on canvas, 1879.*

Left: JE Millais, Portrait of a Girl, *oil on paper, 1857.*

Below: Thomas Brock, Sculpture of JE Millais, *bronze, 1904.*

form of Aestheticism. *The Eve of St Agnes* is an example of this mode: it suggests Pre-Raphaelitism in the title and has Gothic overtones, but his Madeline is in contemporary clothes, a style that became known as artistic dress. One of England's great exponents of this style in painting was JM Whistler, and one can recognize the similarities between his *Symphony in White, No 1: The White Girl* of 1862 and Millais' *The Somnambulist* from 1871. Other paintings of this period, most notably *Esther* (Millais, 1865), successfully combine aspects of Pre-Raphaelitism and Aestheticism.

THE ROYAL ACADEMY

The election of Millais as a full Academician in 1863 was close, brought in by just one vote, a reflection perhaps of his inability to convince detractors of his talent.

In fact, his submission of *The Parable of the Tares* as a diploma picture in 1865 was rejected, a matter that was not resolved until three years later, when the Academy accepted *A Souvenir of Velasquez* in 1868. The work itself is something of a pastiche of Velasquez, but demonstrates Millais' move toward traditional Academic painting.

POPULIST PAINTING

Beginning in the 1860s with *My First Sermon* and continuing to the end of his life, Millais was not averse to creating populist images of children, such as *Cherry Ripe* (1879) and *Bubbles* (1886), which ironically has a Joshua Reynolds quality about it. This latter image (featuring his grandson William) was used as an advertising poster by the Pears Soap Company, which popularized the image well into the 20th century.

It was while at the height of his popularity as one of the foremost artists of the British School that Millais was commissioned to paint leading society figures, including the social reformer Thomas Carlyle (1795–1881), Prime Minister William Gladstone (1809–98) and Sir Henry Irving (1838–1905), the actor, for the Garrick Club.

FINAL YEARS

In his last 20 years, Millais exhibited less at the Academy and more at private galleries, such as the Grosvenor, and in Paris. In 1885 he was created a baronet, the first native-born British artist to be given a hereditary title, and in 1896, following the death of Frederic, Lord Leighton, was elected President of the Royal Academy. He held this title for less than six months before dying at his luxurious home in Kensington, London.

DANTE GABRIEL ROSSETTI

Rossetti was the most controversial of the Pre-Raphaelites, leading a bohemian lifestyle that bordered on eccentricity. A founding member of the Pre-Raphaelite Brotherhood, his art inspired a subsequent generation of Pre-Raphaelites and paved the way for later developments such as Symbolism and Aestheticism. His early paintings are narrative in content, but gave way to more symbolic and spiritual paintings after the 1860s, when he moved to Chelsea and became a mentor for a younger generation. He never became a part of the art establishment, preferring instead to show his work in private galleries. Rossetti was famous as a Lothario and for his depictions of women, sometimes as *femmes fatales* but more often as figures of pathos.

Above: DG Rossetti, Beatrice, Meeting Dante at a Marriage Feast, Denies Him Her Salutation, *watercolour, 1852.*
Left: JE Millais, Portrait Head of Rossetti, *pencil, date unknown.*

THE EARLY YEARS

Raised in a highly creative environment, Dante Gabriel Rossetti was exposed to classical themes from a young age. He sought to augment his education through his translations of Dante, and found artistic encouragement under the tutelage of Ford Madox Brown and William Holman Hunt.

Born to a literary family, Dante Gabriel Rossetti was exposed to the classical themes and ideals that are central to the Pre-Raphaelite ethos from a young age.

PARENTS AND SIBLINGS

Gabriele Rossetti (1783–1854) was a political refugee from Naples who fled to England and became professor of Italian at University College, London. He was married to Frances Polidori (1800–1886), who came from a learned family. They had four children, Dante Gabriel and William Michael, two of the original members of the Pre-Raphaelite Brotherhood, the poet, Christina, and Maria, who wrote a study of Dante Alighieri (1265–1321), as did her father, who was obsessed with the poet. Gabriel Charles Dante Rossetti was the second of those four children, his father giving him the poet's name in homage. Gabriel Rossetti changed his signature to Dante Gabriel Rossetti when the Brotherhood was formed.

Below: DG Rossetti, Portrait of Christina Rossetti, *pastel, 1877.*

EDUCATION

Rossetti's early education was at the renowned King's College School, where his father taught Italian. In 1841, he attended Henry Sass's drawing academy, until enrolled in the Antique School of the Royal Academy in 1845. He was, however, too impetuous for this type of laborious and often tedious training, and seemed far more interested in the literary Romanticism of Walter Scott (1771–1832) and Edgar Allan Poe (1809–49).

TOWARD PRE-RAPHAELITISM

The Rossetti siblings shared their father's passion for Dante and helped translate his work into English. Rossetti was often to be found poring over texts in the British Museum in London. Although he retained his interest in poetry and continued to write, it was as a painter he made his reputation. Having grown tired of the Academy Schools, Rossetti pleaded with the artist Ford Madox

DANTE

Rossetti was fascinated by the poet's Platonic affair with Beatrice Poltinari, a woman with whom Dante had fallen in love on sight when still a boy and whom he glimpsed at regular intervals without getting to know her. Dante was later married to a woman called Gemma, a contractual marriage arranged by her father. The notion of a non-sexual love affair inspired the writing of *La Vita Nuova*, in which prose and poetry are mixed. It was written in 1295, five years after the untimely death of Beatrice aged only 24. Many poets and writers, particularly in the 18th and 19th centuries, were subsequently inspired to write of courtly love.

Brown (1821–93) to take him on as a pupil. Brown had already established a reputation as a history painter in works such as *The First Translation of the Bible into English: Wycliffe Reading His Translation of the New Testament to His Protector, John of Gaunt* (1847–8). Barely five months later, Rossetti was unable to cope with the overbearing Brown and sought refuge at the studio of Holman Hunt. Under his tutelage, Rossetti began his first serious painting, *The Girlhood of Mary Virgin*, completed in 1849.

THE BROTHERHOOD FORMS

At the Academy Schools where he trained, Holman Hunt's closest friend was Millais, who introduced him to Rossetti. Together, the three considered a series of engravings based on the paintings of Benozzo Gozzoli (1421–97), in which the High Renaissance obsession with perspective would be replaced by minute decorative detailing and strong tones that made the work simple and sincere. Three months later, the first full meeting of the Brotherhood took place, with Rossetti suggesting the term in homage to the medieval Romanticism with which he had been, and always would be, associated.

Above: Alphonse Legros, Portrait of William Michael Rossetti, *lithograph, 1864.*

Below: Charles Dodgson, The Rossetti Family, *photograph, 1864.*

Below: Sandro Botticelli, Portrait of Dante Alighieri, *oil on canvas, 15th century.*

THE BROTHERHOOD

Despite being the most outspoken of the founding members of the Brotherhood, Rossetti shied away from presenting his work at the Academy show of 1849. Instead, he sold his work and used the profits to fund a trip around Europe in order to study early Christian art.

Rather than having a formal agenda, the Pre-Raphaelite Brotherhood was established as a group of like-minded detractors of the conventions adopted at the Academy, with Rossetti the most rebellious of the Brothers.

LIKE-MINDED BROTHERS

All of the Pre-Raphaelites despised Sir 'Sloshua' Reynolds, but Rossetti also annotated a copy of Anna Jameson's *The Poetry of Sacred and Legendary Art* with the words 'spit here' each time the work of Peter Paul Rubens (1577–1640) was mentioned. They were all united, however, in their espousal of what William Michael Rossetti propounded 'the study of nature attentively so as to know how to express ideas' and in eschewing 'what is conventional and self-parading and learned by rote'.

Below: Jean Hippolyte Flandrin, Study for the Resurrection of Christ, *oil on card, 1860.*

EXHIBITION 1849

It was agreed by Millais, Hunt and Rossetti that they append the letters 'PRB' to signatures on their works before exhibition, and that they should all offer their work for inclusion in the Royal Academy show of 1849. For their part, Hunt and Millais conformed, but despite Rossetti appending the letters 'PRB' to *The Girlhood of Mary Virgin*, he appeared to have suffered a crisis of confidence and elected instead to show the work at the Free Exhibition in Hyde Park. Rossetti's mother and sister Christina had modelled for the picture, which was sold at the exhibition for 80 guineas. The following year Rossetti again chose not to show his work at the Academy, and his colleagues Hunt and Millais were slated by the critics. This confirmed Rossetti's decision not to show at public exhibitions, and instead to depend on private patronage.

TRAVELS AROUND EUROPE

Using the money from the sale of *The Girlhood of Mary Virgin*, Rossetti decided to visit the Continent to study medieval art, taking Holman Hunt with him. They left for Paris in September 1849, staying in Montmartre. Rossetti wrote to his brother of the works they were seeing, particularly the early Christian art of Fra Angelico (1395–1455) as well as of early Dutch and Flemish painters such as Jan van Eyck (1395–1441). The sight of these paintings had a profound effect on Rossetti, who wrote of the 'astounding finish' and the 'glory of colour' in the works. The two artists are likely to have witnessed the revival of early Christian art in Paris at the hands of artists such as Jean Hippolyte Flandrin (1809–1864), who were painting murals in Parisian churches reminiscent of frescoes by Giotto.

Below: JG Rossetti, Study for the Girlhood of Mary Virgin, *pen ink and wash, c.1849.*

Above: DG Rossetti, Self-portrait, *watercolour, 1849.*

Above right: Hans Memling, Central Panel of the Triptych of St. John the Baptist and St. John the Evangelist, *oil on panel, 1479.*

Right: Tommaso Masaccio, Madonna Casini, *tempera and gold leaf on panel.*

THE PRIMITIVES

On his return to London, Rossetti began work on a new subject inspired by those he had seen on the Continent. The painting in question was *Ecce Ancilla Domini!*, an Annunciation scene that depicts Mary frightened by the appearance of the angel. Like his previous Pre-Raphaelite picture, this work is full of symbolic imagery such as the dove representing the Holy Spirit, and the lily (a symbol of purity) pointing at Mary's womb. In traditional Renaissance pictures, Mary would be wearing blue and/or red, but Rossetti chose white shifts that almost reveal the human form. The artist also included haloes similar to those used in medieval Christian art.

ELIZABETH SIDDAL

The archetypal Pre-Raphaelite beauty, Lizzie Siddal modelled for many of the Brotherhood, although in time she worked solely for, and eventually married, Rossetti. The artist was inconstant in his affections and Lizzie's life was fraught with unhappiness and illness, factors that culminated in her tragic suicide aged just thirty-two.

The Pre-Raphaelites were always seeking models who fulfilled their ideal notion of classical beauty. Many models became favourites of the group, but Elizabeth Siddal is, to this day, the archetypal Pre-Raphaelite beauty.

ROSSETTI'S MUSE

Some time in late 1849 or early 1850, Rossetti met Elizabeth Siddal ('Lizzie'); she had been 'discovered' by Walter Deverell (1827–54) working in a milliner's shop, and had agreed to pose as Viola for his picture *Twelfth Night*. Deverell was enchanted by her pale complexion, red hair and demure look. As a result she was introduced into the Pre-Raphaelite circle and agreed to pose also for Millais' *Ophelia* and Hunt's *A Converted British Family Sheltering a Christian Missionary from the Persecution of the Druids*. Ruskin described her as having 'the look of a Florentine fifteenth-century lady'. Rossetti referred to Lizzie as a 'stunner', a slang expression of the time for a good-looking woman, and after 1852 she agreed to pose exclusively for him. He fell in love with Lizzie and encouraged her to draw and paint under his supervision; she inevitably became his muse and lover, with the nickname 'Guggums'. Rossetti made a number of sketches and watercolours of Lizzie, but used her in few major works; one of these was *Dante Drawing an Angel on the First Anniversary of the Death of Beatrice*, which has been seen by some as parallelling Rossetti (Dante) and Lizzie (Beatrice), particularly in view of her tragic early death in 1862 aged only 32. Lizzie's health was poor and she suffered as a result of her long spells in a bath of water while posing for Millais' *Ophelia*. Rossetti preferred to have her

Right: Elizabeth Siddal, Idea for La Belle Dame Sans Merci, *pencil, date unknown.*

pose reading, painting or just sitting in a chair. Despite their physical intimacy, Rossetti always drew her as though there were a distance between sitter and artist, perhaps to suggest the same platonic intimacy between Dante and Beatrice. It was not until 1860 that he married Lizzie, the intervening years being taken up with other mistresses. Tragically, she was to commit suicide from an overdose of laudanum in 1862, an act for which Rossetti blamed himself; he buried the only copies of his poems with her. He also painted a memorial picture to her entitled *Beata Beatrix*, which he worked on between 1864 and 1870.

THE GERM

Rossetti's contribution to the Pre-Raphaelite journal *The Germ* is significant in offering another outlet for the painter's creative talents. In the first issue he wrote *Hand and Soul*, a fictionalized account of a Florentine 13th-century artist, Chiaro dell'Erma, torn between faith and fame in his pursuit of a career painting religious murals. A woman who reminds him of his integrity as an artist visits him in a dream. The story may mirror the struggles of the Pre-Raphaelites to find artistic integrity, although the conflict in their case was between Ruskinian ideals and their admiration of the archaic.

Above: DG Rossetti, Elizabeth Siddal Reading, *pen and ink, date unknown.*

Above: Paul Rainer, Rossetti and Elizabeth Siddal, *gouache, 20th century.*

Left: DG Rossetti, Elizabeth Siddal, *pen and ink, 1855.*

A NEW STUDIO

In November of 1852, Rossetti left his family home and set up a studio overlooking the River Thames at Blackfriars. The bridge, close by, was the setting for his one and only venture into social realism. The picture, *Found*, was unfinished at his death, but is complete enough to determine its content. It depicts a young woman who has 'fallen', a popular motif in Victorian painting. Other Pre-Raphaelite artists used a similar motif at this time, most notably in Hunt's *The Awakening Conscience*. Fanny Cornforth, a prostitute who accosted Rossetti in the street, modelled for the 'fallen' woman in *Found*, and she too was later to become the artist's mistress. Like Lizzie, Fanny had luxuriant red hair, a key signifier of Pre-Raphaelite women.

RUSKIN'S NEW PROTÉGÉ

John Ruskin's enthusiasm for the Pre-Raphaelite movement had not diminished, despite his estrangement from Millais. He soon became mentor and patron to Rossetti, and focused on bringing out the best in the artist. Rossetti responded by strictly adhering to Ruskinian ideals in his subsequent work.

After the breakdown of his marriage to Effie, John Ruskin's enthusiasm for Millais, his former protégé, understandably waned. Ruskin quickly found a new Pre-Raphaelite to mentor in the form of Rossetti.

JOHN RUSKIN

Francis MacCracken, an early collector of Pre-Raphaelite paintings including Hunt's *The Hireling Shepherd*, introduced Rossetti to Ruskin in 1854. He had shown Ruskin Rossetti's elaborate watercolour *The First Anniversary of the Death of Beatrice*, which the critic described as 'a thoroughly glorious work'. Ruskin, although at times querulous, proved to be a reliable patron over the next few years, purchasing Rossetti's *Arthur's Tomb* in 1855, as well as guiding and coaxing other buyers toward the artist's work. Most importantly, he brought the best out of Rossetti by reprimanding him if he produced inadequate work. In Rossetti's version of *The Annunciation*, painted in 1855, the artist adhered closely to the tenets of Ruskinian thought and eschewed all notions of what Ruskin termed 'the idea of a graceful princess crowned with gems' in his depiction of the Virgin Mary. Ruskin also persuaded Rossetti to begin teaching at the Working Men's College in London at the beginning of 1855, to allow him to express his creative ideas in a public arena.

DANTE AND BEATRICE

The poet Dante's greatest work is the *Divine Comedy*, written between 1308 and his death in 1321. It is an imagined journey into an afterlife in which the writer travels through the Inferno (Hell) and on to Purgatory, before finally reaching Paradise. It is considered an allegory of the spiritual journey one makes toward God. The Roman poet Virgil takes Dante on the first two

stages of the journey, but it is Beatrice, the spiritual courtly love of his childhood, who takes him on the last phase toward Paradise. Several incidents in the *Divine Comedy* inspired Rossetti, as they had inspired the earlier 19th-century painter and poet, William Blake, whose work was well known to the artist's brother, William Michael Rossetti. The visual arts were only one manifestation of Dante's influence at this time: Franz Liszt's symphony of the same name was first performed in 1856, and Honoré de Balzac's literary version *La Comédie Humaine*, was published in 1849. Another character in the *Divine Comedy* is Francesca da

Above: DG Rossetti, The Salutation of Beatrice in Eden, *watercolour, 1850–54.*

Rimini, who tells Dante of her lust for a man called Paolo that caused his violent death at the hands of his brother Giovanni. Francesca maintained that her lust was aroused by reading the adulterous stories about the medieval knight Sir Lancelot and Queen Guinevere. Rossetti used motifs from both Dante's work and Arthurian legend as inspirations for his pictures. However, his passion was for Beatrice, personified by his muse Elizabeth Siddal. In *The Salutation of Beatrice in Eden* (1850–4), Rossetti depicts Dante paying

Right: DG Rossetti, Dante's Dream, *pencil, 1874.*

homage to Beatrice while he is still in Purgatory. The artist remains faithful to Ruskinian detail, depicting Beatrice in a green mantle over a red dress, authentic to the *Divine Comedy* text, and using a death mask of Dante (which was in Rossetti's possession) to represent the features of the poet accurately. This small watercolour was intended to have been one of a pair in a diptych. The project was abandoned and not completed until 1854. For a while, the painting was in the collection of Philip Webb, the Arts and Crafts architect and designer who would later work with Rossetti under the direction of William Morris. This may be because the two small watercolours of the diptych originally flanked a larger centrepiece oil painting in a room set, *Dantis Amor,* as a proposed design for a decorative panel on a cabinet by Morris and Webb.

Above: W & D Downey, Rossetti, Ruskin and Bell Scott, *photograph, date unknown.*

Left: DG Rossetti, Dante in Meditation, *pen and ink, c.1852.*

ARTHURIAN LEGEND

Rossetti's interest in medieval romanticism and Arthurian legend was shared by Lizzie Siddal, allowing them to increase their bond and work side-by-side as artists. These concepts also struck a chord with William Morris, who asked Rossetti to contribute to the painting of the ceiling of Oxford University's Debating Hall.

Under Rossetti's tutelage, Lizzie Siddal had become an accomplished artist in her own right. The couple's mutual interest in medieval romanticism allowed their relationship to transcend that of painter and muse, and work together as artists.

A COMMON INTEREST

Rossetti and Siddal both shared a passion for Arthurian legend. After reading an 1817 edition of the book *Le Morte d'Arthur*, written by Sir Thomas Malory in the 15th century, Rossetti produced the painting *Arthur's Tomb*, subtitled *The Last Meeting of*

Lancelot and Guinevere, later sold to Ruskin. The title refers to a passage in Malory's book in which Lancelot and Guinevere's adulterous affair has ended, and the two are remorseful over the death of King Arthur, with Guinevere becoming a nun in atonement. Rossetti and Lizzie worked together on *The Quest of the Holy Grail*, a composition first created by Lizzie, also inspired by Malory, but probably based on Tennyson's poem on Sir Galahad. Like the other Pre-Raphaelite artists, Rossetti was asked to contribute drawings for the forthcoming book of Tennyson's poems to be published by

Edward Moxon (1801–58). Rossetti was keen to also include Lizzie in the project, and completed four of her drawings for the book, including *Sir Galahad at the Ruined Chapel*. In the watercolour version made three years later, Rossetti positioned Sir Galahad against a background that is more lively and vibrant, reminiscent of a design for a tapestry, which is appropriate given that he was embarking on a new aspect of his career, that of design.

Below: DG Rossetti, Sir Lancelot in the Queen's Bedchamber, *pen, ink and watercolour, 1857.*

Left: Elizabeth Siddal, The Lady of Shalott, *ink on paper, 1853.*

OXFORD PROJECT

Rossetti was given the opportunity to express his vision of the Arthurian legends on a grand scale, when he was asked by Morris to help paint the vaulted ceiling of the Debating Hall at the Oxford Union (now the library) with depictions from Malory's *Le Morte d'Arthur.* Other artists involved included Burne-Jones, Spencer Stanhope (1829–1908), Arthur Hughes (1832–1915) and, of course, Morris. Rossetti only completed one bay based on Sir Lancelot's search for the Holy Grail, before funding dried up, time ran out and the work remained unfinished. However, Arthurian legend and medievalism remained main subjects in the work of the second generation of Pre-Raphaelites, led by Rossetti, into the 1860s.

THE ARDOUR FOR LIZZIE COOLS

At the time of the Oxford project, Lizzie was ill, suffering from the mental illness that was to dog her until her death in 1862. Her relationship with Rossetti had cooled and she travelled around France, not returning to England until 1860, when she married the artist. Meanwhile, however, he had become enamoured of Jane Burden, whom he had seen in London and asked to pose as Queen Guinevere.

WILLIAM MORRIS

Destined for ordination as a priest, William Morris began studying at Exeter College, Oxford, in 1852.
He and his fellow student Edward Burne-Jones (1833–1898) were keen to embrace the new vision of Tractarianism (also known as the Oxford Movement), which opposed the tendency to simplify worship in the Anglican church and sought to re-establish many of the medieval traditions. Morris was disappointed at the lack of public support, and was inspired to use his

Above: DG Rossetti, Sir Galahad at the Ruined Chapel, *watercolour, 1859.*

artistic talents to combat what he saw as a decline of moral and aesthetic values. On seeing Rossetti's painting *The First Anniversary of the Death of Beatrice,* he was immediately taken with the notions of medieval romanticism, which he believed could help the tractarians in their cause.

Right: DG Rossetti, Glorious Gwendolen's Golden Hair, *painted chair, 1856–7.*

A WANDERING EYE

Rossetti's relationship with Lizzie Siddal was fraught with complications, which were catalysed by her ailing health and his inconstant affections. While Lizzie was convalescing in France, Rossetti became enamoured of several other women, but ultimately went back to Lizzie upon her return.

Rossetti was always looking out for new models, and his fascination with female beauty extended beyond his art.

FANNY CORNFORTH

In 1858, a prostitute named Sarah Cox (1835–1906), who used the working name of Fanny Cornforth, solicited Rossetti in the street. At this time Rossetti was beginning to explore the idea of feminine beauty without literary or religious significance. In *Fazio's Mistress* (based on an Italian poem translated by Rossetti), for example, he depicted Fanny brushing and plaiting her hair. She appears again in *Fair Rosamund*, another study of feminine beauty, and although based on a real person with a tragic story there is no narrative in the painting. Rossetti's attachment to Fanny in the absence of Lizzie blossomed into an affair that was kept fairly discreet because of her class. She unfortunately gained weight during their ten-year relationship, the artist referring to her as 'Dear Elephant' in his letters.

JANE BURDEN

Another 'stunner' from a humble working-class background was Jane Burden (1839–1914). She was barely literate and was probably destined for life in service before she met Rossetti, William Morris and Burne-Jones in the summer of 1857, in Oxford, where she lived.

Morris immediately fell in love with her and they became engaged, marrying in April 1859. They moved into the 'Palace of Art', designed by the Arts and Crafts architect Philip Webb and furnished by friends of theirs including Rossetti. It would be several more years before Jane and Rossetti became more intimate in their friendship, but the seeds had already been sown.

Above: DG Rossetti, Jane Morris, *pencil, 1857.*

Left: DG Rossetti, Fanny Cornforth (Study for Fair Rosamund), *coloured chalk, 1861.*

Above: DG Rossetti, Elizabeth Siddal, *pencil, c.1860.*

rebound. Ruskin visited the newly married couple in September to offer his congratulations. There were several other marriages at this time among their circle, including, Burne-Jones. On their return to London, the Rossettis rented a cottage in Hampstead close to the Madox Browns. The house was small and so Rossetti kept on his studio at Blackfriars and commuted. Within a short time, Lizzie became pregnant and they moved back to Rossetti's refurbished bachelor flat to house the expected baby. Tragically, Lizzie became ill again prior to the birth and in May 1861 the child was stillborn. Within a few months, Lizzie too died from an overdose of laudanum, leaving a suicide note waiting for Rossetti when he returned home one evening from teaching at the Working Men's College. She was only 32 and pregnant again. Rossetti was devastated, writing several poems about his loss and creating one of his best-known works, *Beata Beatrix*, as a memorial to her.

MARRIAGE TO LIZZIE

Lizzie returned to England from her travels in early 1860 and she was finally married to Rossetti in May. They honeymooned in Paris, where he worked on a complex pen and ink drawing, *How They Met Themselves*, depicting a medieval couple walking in the woods confronted by their doppelgängers as the harbingers of death. It has been suggested that perhaps the motive for such a macabre subject being painted on a honeymoon was that Rossetti was seeking to exorcise the demons that had plagued their on-off relationship in previous years. It may also have been prophetic of the tragic outcome less than two years later, one which perhaps Rossetti had feared all along. On hearing the news of the marriage, Fanny Cornforth was said to be heartbroken, and within a few months had married on the

Right: DG Rossetti, Mary Magdalene at the Door, *pen and ink, 1853–9.*

LIFE AFTER LIZZIE

After Lizzie's death, Rossetti found solace and diversion in the formation of 'The Firm', a joint venture with William Morris and other eminent Pre-Raphaelites. He also travelled around Europe, finding inspiration for his art in the works of Édouard Manet and James McNeill Whistler.

Above: DG Rossetti, Portrait of Swinburne, *watercolour, 1861.*

Above: DG Rossetti, The Visitation, *stained glass, 1861.*

By 1861, Rossetti had become the leader of the second wave of Pre-Raphaelitism, with William Morris as one of his disciples. Morris had recognized by this time that his talents lay in design rather than as a fine artist, and he sought to exploit these talents to further the Pre-Raphaelite cause.

MORRIS, MARSHALL, FAULKNER & COMPANY

Morris was surrounded by a wealth of talent in Philip Webb the architect, Burne-Jones, Madox Brown and Rossetti as painters and designers; he founded the firm of Morris, Marshall, Faulkner & Company ('The Firm'),

including his friends as partners. He produced a pamphlet to advertise their services that stated: 'They will be able to undertake any species of decoration, mural or otherwise, from pictures, properly so-called, down to the consideration of the smallest work susceptible of art beauty.'

Early on, they specialized in designing stained glass for the burgeoning of Gothic Revival churches being built at the time. Although medieval in concept, their designs were richer in colour and simpler in layout.

Morris himself believed that any artist could develop their talents in order to counteract some of the deplorable designs being executed, particularly in furniture, at this time, mainly at the hands of untrained designers. Morris's own forte was as a designer of tapestries and wall coverings, incorporating flat patterns recalling medieval simplicity. Within ten years, his firm, later renamed Morris & Co, had become synonymous with beautiful household furnishings that were 'neat, not gaudy'.

Above: Édouard Manet, Olympia, *oil on canvas, 1863.*

Below right: DG Rossetti, Rossetti Lamenting the Death of his Wombat, *pen and ink on paper, 1869.*

CHELSEA

Following Lizzie's death, Rossetti moved to Tudor House in Chelsea, a grand house overlooking the River Thames. Rossetti was now regularly selling his paintings and had become relatively wealthy. In 1865, Rossetti started to buy exotic animals, including a wombat, a kangaroo, and a peacock. His housekeeper at the time was Fanny Cornforth, who lodged nearby. She continued to pose for him until 1865, when he met Alexa Wilding, whom Rossetti had stopped in the street and persuaded to pose for him. She became, for him, as his brother William said, the 'Venetian ideal of female beauty'. It appears that Rossetti was not intimate with Alexa, liking her dream-like looks rather than her company. Alexa aspired to a stage career, and also posed for Burne-Jones, most notably in his *The Blessed Demozel*.

TRAVELS TO EUROPE

In 1863, Rossetti travelled with his brother to the Low Countries, visiting Ghent, Bruges and Antwerp and starting a collection of blue and white porcelain. He spent several months in the area before travelling to Paris and meeting Édouard Manet (1833–1883) in November. Manet had caused a scandal when exhibiting *Le Déjeuner sur l'Herbe* at the Salon des Refusés in Paris earlier that year, a picture that shows two fully clothed men picknicking with a completely naked woman. At the same exhibition was Whistler's *Symphony in White No 1: The White Girl*, another painting too controversial for the French Royal Academy. On visiting Manet's studio, it seems likely that Rossetti saw *Olympia*, which, although completed in 1863, was not exhibited for another two years, and was almost universally condemned for its outrageous frankness. It seems likely that these pictures influenced Rossetti's own work *The Beloved* in 1865.

ILLNESS AND INFATUATION

In the years after Lizzie's death, Rossetti suffered from bouts of depression and melancholia, worsened by the firm belief that he was losing his sight. He found relief, and a new muse, in the form of Jane Morris, to whom he grew very attached, as well as in his growing collections of Japanese art and porcelain.

Having established 'The Firm's offices in Red Lion Square, in central London, William and Jane moved from the 'Palace of Art', outside London, back to the city and lived above the premises. This brought Jane back into regular contact with Rossetti.

JANE MORRIS

Soon after the Morrises return to London, Rossetti began to use Jane as a model again, starting by commissioning a series of photographs of her in his garden in Chelsea. They corresponded regularly, with Rossetti addressing his letters to 'My dear Janey' and signing himself 'Your affectionate Gabriel'. In fact, both she and Rossetti were unwell. In June of 1869, Jane went to Germany to take the waters at Bad Ems, a spa town on the Rhine. Rossetti and Jane continued corresponding while she was away in Germany and he was convalescing in Scotland.

ROSSETTI'S ILLNESS

By 1867, Rossetti was suffering from eyesight problems, although there was apparently nothing physically wrong. He also had severe bouts of melancholia and depression that began in the wake

Below: Walter Greaves, Whistler in the Cremorne Gardens, *watercolour, 1869.*

of Lizzie's tragic death. He had tried to exorcise his guilt through the painting of *Beata Beatrix*, on which he worked between 1864 and 1870. He was morose in the company of his friends and even spoke of suicide. In the autumn of 1868, he travelled to Ayrshire with his friend William Bell Scott (1811–90) to recuperate. They stayed at Penkhill Castle, the home of Miss Boyd, a friend of Scott and an amateur painter herself. Here he appears to have acquired the taste for malt whisky; before this he only drank wine. In the following year, he returned to Penkhill with thoughts about re-establishing himself as a poet. On the death of Lizzie, he had placed the only copies of his poems in her coffin, and was persuaded by friends that he should seek their retrieval. After a special dispensation from the Home Secretary, Henry Bruce (1815–95), he was finally given permission for Lizzie's disinterment in October 1869.

Below: Chinese blue and white brushpot, porcelain, c.1640.

ROSSETTI THE COLLECTOR

On moving to Chelsea, apart from his menagerie, Rossetti had begun a number of collections, of exotic artefacts from Asia. During the 1860s, Japanese woodblock prints were flooding the market and became a source of inspiration for European artists, particularly in Paris and London. The simple lines, flat areas of colour and lack of perspective entranced them. Rossetti also collected blue and white Japanese and Chinese porcelain, as did his near neighbour Whistler. This type of porcelain was already popular in Britain, but it was only after the trade embargoes had been lifted in Japan in the 1850s that authentic Japanese artefacts were again allowed into Britain after 200 years. The prints, originally only seen in Britain as wrapping material for the porcelain, became collectable as well, starting a new trend in so-called *Japonisme* in Britain and France.

Below: DG Rossetti, Jane Morris, *pencil, 1861.*

Above: Henry Treffry Dunn, Calliope Coronio, *after Dante Gabriel Rossetti, pastel, 1869.*

It was Scott who first noticed that Rossetti's illness was exacerbated by his obsession with Jane. In addition, Rossetti was suffering from insomnia, which he tried to treat with a combination of whisky and chloral, a recently developed narcotic drug with hypnotic powers.

During his illnesses, then and later, Henry Treffry Dunn (1838–97), Rossetti's studio assistant, undertook some of his master's work. Rossetti's biographer, Evelyn Waugh (1903–66), suggests that Rossetti maintained his income at this time by producing a steady flow of replicas that may well have been undertaken by Dunn.

ROSSETTI THE POET

Spurred on by his grief at Lizzie's death, Rossetti explored themes of love and loss through his poetry. The poems were generally well received upon publication, but Rossetti's fragile nerves drove him to attempt suicide after he was criticized for the overtly sensual nature of his work.

Following the disinterment of Lizzie's coffin, Rossetti managed to retrieve the only copies of his poetry. After drying and disinfecting them, they were updated, amended and compiled into an anthology, published in April 1870.

POETRY

By 1870 Rossetti had recuperated from his illness and was excited about his new forays into poetry. He was not disappointed as the book was well received, although the reviews were mainly by his friends and family, for example in *The Fortnightly Review* by Algernon Swinburne, and in *The Athenaeum* by his brother William. The poems deal with the sense of loss, the realization of mortality and the transience of love. *Stillborn Love*, for example, a sonnet based on his and Lizzie's own experience, begins:

The hour which might have been
 yet might not be,
Which man's and woman's heart
 conceived and bore
Yet whereof life was barren.

The emphasis in *The One Hope* is on Rossetti's own mortality:

When vain desire at last and
 vain regret
Go hand in hand to death,
 and all is vain
What shall assuage the
 unforgotten pain
And teach the unforgetful to forget?

Left: Frontispiece to News from Nowhere, *woodcut, 1892.*

THIS IS THE PICTURE OF THE OLD HOUSE BY THE THAMES TO WHICH THE PEOPLE OF THIS STORY WENT HEREAFTER FOLLOWS THE BOOK IT-SELF WHICH IS CALLED NEWS FROM NOWHERE OR AN EPOCH OF REST & IS WRITTEN BY WILLIAM MORRIS

KELMSCOTT MANOR

William Morris and Rossetti jointly took out a lease on Kelmscott Manor, a Tudor house with later additions in the Oxfordshire countryside, close to the source of the River Thames, in 1871. Morris was enamoured of its original condition and its craftsmanship. Rossetti spent that summer at Kelmscott in the company of Jane. It has been suggested that Rossetti had begun an affair with Jane in 1869, and that Morris arranged Kelmscott in order that it could be conducted with propriety. However, there is little evidence that they were actually lovers at all. Morris was away for that summer in Iceland, knowing that he would be leaving them together. Rossetti continued to spend time at Kelmscott with Jane until 1874, when he left and sold his interest in 'The Firm', the relationship between him and Morris having become untenable.

to recuperate. In September he left for Kelmscott, where he stayed with Jane for the next two years. Jane posed for many of Rossetti's famous paintings, such as *Proserpine* and *Astarte Syriaca*, which both depict the luxuriant dark hair of his model and herald his move away from allegory to a depiction of passion and eroticism, enlivened by the gorgeous costumes she wore. This marks the high point of Rossetti's *oeuvre*.

Above: DG Rossetti, A Study for 'The Bower Meadow', *pen and ink, date unknown.*

THE 'FLESHY' SCANDAL

In October 1871, Rossetti was the subject of an attack in the *Contemporary Review* which referred to the 'Fleshy' school of poetry. Robert Buchanan (1841–1901) wrote the article, and later expanded his criticism into a pamphlet entitled *The Fleshy School of Poetry and other Phenomena*. He saw Rossetti's poems as overly sensuous and morally decadent, accusing him of pursuing 'fleshiness as [the] distinct and supreme end of poetic and pictorial art'. Given Rossetti's vulnerable state at this time, it was not surprising that he attempted suicide, in June 1872, by swallowing an entire phial of laudanum. He was initially cared for by Madox Brown, who took him to Scotland

Right: DG Rossetti, Study for David (William Morris), *pencil, 1859–62.*

ROSSETTI'S FINAL YEARS

In the final years of Rosetti's life he grew increasingly isolated, alienating his friends and also the artistic establishment as a whole. His melancholy was further fuelled by the dire state of his finances, which meant that he was forced to sell off his beloved collections to raise money.

The last years of Rossetti's life were lonely ones, as he removed himself from society and steadily became more reclusive. His withdrawal from public life was also evident in his art, as he abandoned his Pre-Raphaelite ideals and refused to exhibit at an important new gallery.

AFTERMATH OF KELMSCOTT

Although Jane continued to sit for Rossetti, he had turned his back on Kelmscott and William Morris after 1874. His finances had been repaired largely through the intervention of his friends, Bell Scott and Madox Brown, who, for example, had arranged to sell his collection of blue and white china to raise funds. He returned to Tudor House in the summer of 1874, a rather bleak and empty home now devoid of his collections. With its painful memories, Rossetti decided to leave London and rented a house at Bognor on the south coast, where he remained until the spring of the following year.

A NEW GALLERY

The wealthy and influential Sir Coutts Lindsay (1824–1913) and his wife Blanche opened the Grosvenor Gallery in London's Bond St in 1877. They had hoped to attract the second generation of Pre-Raphaelites, as well as followers of the emerging Aesthetic movement, whose credo was 'art for art's sake', and who included Whistler and Burne-Jones. Both Rossetti and Madox Brown were approached but declined to show their work. This act may well have been the final nail in the coffin of Pre-Raphaelitism as a coherent art movement. Rossetti in particular had long since lost interest in the Pre-Raphaelite ideals.

Above: English School, The Grosvenor Gallery, *Engraving, 1877.*

FURTHER ILLNESS AND ISOLATION

In the summer of 1877, Rossetti was taken ill again, this time with a urinary ailment which left him bedridden for two months. He was despairing again, and turned to chloral and alcohol. His work varied in quality as he vacillated between an intoxicated state and coherence. Nevertheless, *Astarte Syriaca*, painted between 1875 and 1877, is an exemplar of the synthesis between his painting and poetry:

Mystery: lo! betwixt the sun and moon
Astarte of the Syrians: Venus, Queen
Ere Aphrodite was. In silver sheen
Her twofold girdle clasps the infinite boon
Of bliss whereof the heaven and earth commune…

Right: DG Rossetti, Head of a Woman Called Ruth, *chalk on paper, 1876.*

At Tudor House, Rossetti became more reclusive. He had lost contact with his old Pre-Raphaelite friends but was visited by other artists. His main supporters were his brother William and the poet Theodore Watts-Dunton (1832–1914).

FINAL MONTHS

One visitor of Rossetti's from September 1880 was the future novelist Hall Caine (1853–1931). As a young man he had read Rossetti's poems and, in 1881, went to work for him as a secretary and general factotum. In autumn, Rossetti and Caine went to Penrith in Cumbria along with Fanny Schott (formerly Cornforth). It was a dreadful month for Rossetti, as he was badgered by Fanny to remember her in his will. Rossetti suffered a stroke in December and went to Birchington on Sea to recover, but he died there on 9 April 1882, with Caine and his brother William by his side. He was buried in the local churchyard.

Above: DG Rossetti, The Blessed Damozel, *oil on canvas, 1875–9.*

Left: Frederick Shields, The Dead Rossetti, *chalk on paper, 1882.*

W Holman Hunt

WILLIAM HOLMAN HUNT

Hunt's biographer, Anne Clark Amor, refers to the artist as 'the true Pre-Raphaelite' in recognition of his unwavering loyalty to the Brotherhood's principles. He was one of the original members, and continued painting in that aesthetic until 1910, longer than any of the other members, or their followers. He came from a working-class background and had great difficulty persuading his father to accept his choice of career as an artist. He became linked with the Pre-Raphaelites early on, but his lack of a personal fortune made his early years difficult. It was not long, however, before he found sympathetic patrons to buy his work. He became a very religious and spiritual person, and sought 'truth to nature' in the Holy Land in order that his paintings could be imbued with a sense of religious truth relevant to his own era, rather than as a historical narrative.

Above: WH Hunt, Eve of St Agnes, *oil on panel, 1847–57.*
Left: WH Hunt, Self-portrait, *tinted lithograph, 1880.*

HUNT'S EARLY YEARS

Born to pragmatic parents, William Holman Hunt was dissuaded from pursuing a career as an artist and pushed toward an occupation that would provide a more reliable income. Hunt's artistic nature triumphed over circumstance when he received encouragement from outside the family sphere.

Holman Hunt's upbringing by business-minded parents had not made him a natural candidate to embark on an artistic career. His passion and talent triumphed over circumstance, however, and he was soon established at the Royal Academy Schools.

FAMILY BACKGROUND

When Sarah Hobman married William Hunt in 1822, it was considered that she had married beneath her status. Her father was a wealthy horse-breeder who had gambled away his fortune, although he had provided well for his three sons. William's father, by contrast, was manager of a warehouse in the City of London. On 2 April 1827, Sarah gave birth to their first son, named William, after his father, and Hobman after his mother's brother. However, owing to a spelling error on the baptismal certificate, the young boy was thereafter known as William Holman Hunt. The young William often went

Above: WH Hunt, Study of a Bloodhound, oil over pencil, 1848.

with his father to work, gaining a strong sense of business procedure. At the age of eight he was sent to boarding school, where his father often visited him. During the holidays he often stayed with his wealthy uncle William Hobman, who owned a farm in Surrey. Here, he developed a taste for the outdoor life and sport, becoming very proficient in boxing. When Hunt was 12, he told his father he wanted to be an artist.

His father reminded him of the pitfalls of such a precarious career, urging him to leave school immediately and go to work in the warehouse, hoping that the boy would lose interest in art.

Left: WH Hunt, Old Church, Ewell, oil on canvas, 1847.

The young Hunt found a job for himself as an office clerk, and the proprietor of this business, an amateur artist himself, encouraged him to pursue his interest. Hunt attended evening classes in drawing and spent time studying paintings in the National Gallery. Finally, his father relented toward his son's aspirations, providing him with a small studio and writing a letter of introduction to the Royal Academy to enable him to attend the lectures there.

THE ACADEMY SCHOOLS

In 1843, Hunt was sketching at the British Museum when the rising star of the Academy Schools, John Everett Millais, approached him. Following his advice, Hunt submitted a drawing to the Academy Schools and was accepted as a probationer in July 1844, to begin his studies the following year. When they met again in January, Hunt was invited to Millais' own studio in Gower Street. Despite their social inequality, Hunt was made very welcome by Millais' parents, especially his mother, who offered to help him with subjects for painting. This could not have been more at odds with the indifference to art in his own parental home. However, before long, Hunt's father was invited to the Millais' house and saw the artistic world in a new light. He finally agreed to support the young Holman (as he now wanted to be known) in his chosen career and offered him financial help.

FIRST EXHIBITIONS

Hunt exhibited *Little Nell and Her Grandfather*, based on Dickens's *The Old Curiosity Shop*, at the British Institution in 1846. In the same year, he also submitted *Hark* to the Royal Academy exhibition. Both pictures displayed a sentimentality that appealed to the Victorian mind, and Hunt fully exploited the naivety and innocence in the face of his seven-year old sister Emily.

At the time he left school, Hunt had had very little literary education, but he was now making up for this by avidly reading the novels of, among others, Dickens and Walter Scott.

Above: WH Hunt, Little Nell and Her Grandfather, *oil on canvas, 1846.*

His first religious picture was *Christ and the Two Marys*, and he visited Kew Gardens especially so that he could see some palm trees for reference material.

At this time he borrowed, a copy of John Ruskin's *Modern Painters* for 24 hours only. After sitting up all night to read it, he was set on a new course. His next painting was *The Flight of Madeline and Porphyro During the Drunkenness Attending the Revelry*, inspired by Keats's poem *The Eve of St Agnes*. This was his first Pre-Raphaelite work, exhibited at the Royal Academy several months before he met Rossetti and the Brotherhood was formed.

Above: Anonymous, Holman Hunt and Ruskin, *photograph, date unknown.*

EARLY PATRONAGE

Holman Hunt found common aesthetic ground with Millais and Rossetti, and in 1848 the three friends founded the Pre-Raphaelite Brotherhood. Rossetti's and Millais' wealthy social and familial connections allowed them to recommend Holman Hunt to potential patrons, raising his profile in the process.

Hunt, Millais and Rossetti, were the three originators of the Brotherhood in 1848. Previously, Hunt and Millais had discussed the deterioration of Western painting and agreed that it began with Raphael's *Transfiguration*, executed at the end of the artist's life. They expressed this view to their fellow students at the Academy School, one of whom then stated that they must therefore be 'Pre-Raphaelites'.

FIRST STEPS

Hunt's first picture as a member of the Brotherhood, exhibited at the Royal Academy exhibition of 1849, was *Rienzi Vowing to Obtain Justice for the Death of His Young Brother, Slain in a Skirmish Between the Colonna and Orsini Factions*. Like Millais' *Isabella*, exhibited at the same time, it bore the initials PRB on the canvas, Hunt's only painting to do so. It was accompanied by a citation from Bulwer Lytton's novel *Rienzi, the Last of the Tribunes*. Hunt's models were

Rossetti and his brother William as the key protagonists, Rienzi and Adrian. Reception of the picture was mixed but Lytton himself praised it, seeing it as 'full of genius and promise'.

PAINTING THE LANDSCAPE

Early paintings by Hunt show that he understood the landscape and how to paint it. Having read Ruskin he was inspired to adopt his central tenet of 'truth to nature' in his paintings. *Love at First Sight* from 1848 demonstrates this. The site is Blackheath Common in south-east London, and it was originally intended as a painted background study for a larger picture. The habit of painting the background landscape to a figurative painting *en plein air* began in earnest at this time, and was continued for much of his career. The locations were varied but were generally in the then suburbs of London such as Clapham, and in the Surrey countryside at Ewell and Worcester Park.

CHARTISM

In April 1848, Hunt and Millais joined the Chartist march through London to Kennington Common, just south of the Thames. Chartism had begun ten years earlier with the 'People's Charter', the first official organized working-class labour movement in the world. The Charter sought to give working-class people the vote, rather than just those who owned property. A series of industrial strikes and protests had taken place in the intervening years, but the rally in 1848 was the largest with an estimated 150,000 people seeking to support the franchise. Victorian society's malaise and hypocrisy came increasingly under Hunt's scrutiny, and he produced a number of pictures that comment on these themes.

Above: JE Millais, Portrait of Thomas Combe, *oil on panel, 1850.*

Left: Frederick Sandys, The Old Chartist, *engraving, 1909.*

Above: WH Hunt, Love at First Sight, *oil on panel, 1848.*

Right: Elliott and Fry, Portraits of Ruskin and Hunt, *photograph, date unknown.*

ROSSETTI AND A NEW STUDIO

Rossetti and Hunt became firm friends after Rossetti admired his painting *The Eve of St Agnes* at the 1848 Royal Academy exhibition. Hunt, having received payment for *Rienzi* after the Academy exhibition the following year, decided to travel with Rossetti to France, the first time that Hunt had ever left the country. The two artists enjoyed each other's company, seeking out the art galleries first in Paris and later in Ghent and Bruges. On his return to London, Hunt secured a new studio in Chelsea that was to be his home as well.

THOMAS COMBE

One of the earliest and most important patrons of Pre-Raphaelite art was Thomas Combe, the owner of the Clarendon Press in Oxford. It was Millais that first sang Hunt's praises to Combe, persuading him to buy his work

A Converted British Family Sheltering a Christian Missionary from the Persecution of the Druids, a large-scale history painting, for £126 (about £11,000 today). This was badly needed as many of Hunt's possessions were at the pawnbroker and his clothes were mostly beyond repair.

DEVELOPING RELATIONSHIPS

Despite the initial camaraderie between Holman Hunt and his Pre-Raphaelite Brothers, cracks soon began to develop and petty grievances arose within the Brotherhood. Hunt struggled to pay Annie Miller, his new model, and his lack of income made him question his choice of career as an artist.

The differing social backgrounds of the Brotherhood, particularly between Hunt and Rossetti, did not hamper their personal relationships. However, Hunt's relative poverty made it difficult for him to commit fully to the Pre-Raphaelite cause, making it harder for him to earn a living and almost causing him to abandon his career as a painter altogether.

SEVENOAKS

With a friendship firmly cemented in the wake of the adverse publicity at the 1849 Academy exhibition, and having travelled in Europe, Hunt and Rossetti worked together in the autumn of that year at Sevenoaks in Kent. Hunt was working on *Valentine Rescuing Sylvia from Proteus*, a depiction from Shakespeare's *Two Gentlemen of Verona*. The weather was poor and, to make matters worse, Lizzie Siddal had failed to turn up and sit for Hunt as Sylvia, apparently angry at a practical joke Hunt had performed some weeks earlier. Eventually she agreed to sit for him on his return to London to create the picture, which would be shown at the Academy Exhibition in 1851.

SOCIAL MATTERS

Personality clashes sometimes caused friction between the Brothers. James Collinson had resigned, as he felt that his membership was at odds with his Catholic faith, and it was proposed that his place be given to Walter Deverell. Hunt objected to this on a point of order that annoyed the other Brothers. Hunt and Rossetti also had problems sharing a

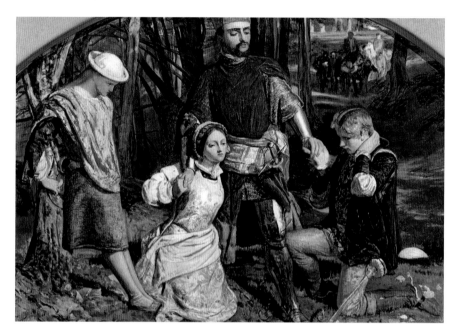

Above right: WH Hunt, Valentine Rescuing Sylvia *from Proteus, oil on canvas, 1850–1.*

Right: DG Rossetti, Annie Miller, pen and ink, date unknown.

Above: WH Hunt, The Light of the World, *oil on canvas, 1857.*

studio: though Hunt would patiently help his friend in his often frustrated attempts to achieve 'truth to nature', he found it difficult to accept when Rossetti turned up at the studio with friends and expect Hunt to cater for them.

SITTERS WANTED

The Brotherhood were constantly on the look-out for 'stunners' to act as sitters, and were to be found walking the streets of London looking for suitable models to pose for them. At some time in early 1851, Hunt encountered his own 'stunner': a 15-year-old girl with luxuriant blonde hair called Annie Miller. She had worked in a public house and had also been a prostitute. She was socially inept, dirty, vulgar and illiterate, but Hunt proudly showed Annie off to his friends who also wanted to use her as a model.

PENURY

Hunt continued to struggle financially. The situation had become so bad that he seriously considered giving up painting altogether, and even contemplated training as a cattle farmer and emigrating to Australia. However, Millais came to his rescue. In June 1851, Hunt and Millais moved to Kingston in Surrey. Hunt began his picture *The Hireling Shepherd* here, using the local landscape as background. He also began sketching designs for *The Light of the World*; this painting engaged Hunt for two years. Meanwhile, Hunt had gained another patron, Thomas Fairbairn (1823–91), a wealthy industrialist.

A SOCIAL CONSCIENCE

A number of artists were concerned about aspects of Victorian life such as deprivation, injustice and the hypocrisy of its social mores. Hunt began one of his most controversial paintings, *The Awakening Conscience*, in 1853. It depicts the moment in a young woman's life when she becomes aware of being a kept woman. The picture is full of symbolism, such as the cat tormenting the bird, an allegory of the relationship between the man and his mistress. Thomas Fairbairn purchased the picture.

Below: WH Hunt, Mrs Fairbairn and Her Children, *oil on canvas, 1864.*

THE HOLY LAND

William Holman Hunt's religious paintings garnered him mixed reviews, leading him to travel to the Holy Land for inspiration. Here, he produced several paintings but, after exposing the corruption of the local Anglican community, he became disillusioned with evangelical religion as a whole.

Hunt was interested in the spirituality of religion, having witnessed the rise of High Anglicanism in Oxford in 1852 while staying with Thomas Combe, and he read the bible enthusiastically. Reaction to his early religious paintings was mixed, leading him to visit the Holy Land looking for inspiration for his work.

RELIGIOUS PAINTINGS

Hunt's first exhibited religious work was *The Light of the World*, shown at the Academy in 1854. The picture received criticism for its realism, which, according to some, negated its spiritual quality.

Thomas Carlyle, a close friend of Ruskin and a highly regarded social commentator, who had admired Hunt's *The Hireling Shepherd*, visited the artist at his studio in order to see *The Light of the World* and unfortunately described it as 'mere papistical fantasy'. Ruskin came to Hunt's rescue, explaining the symbolism of the picture and calling it 'one of the very noblest works of sacred art'.

Below: WH Hunt, Arab Resting by a Stream, *watercolour, 1854.*

THE HOLY LAND

The public's mixed reaction to his religious paintings made Hunt decide to visit the Holy Land. His Academy paintings were selling well and he had been commissioned to execute others. At the end of 1854, he therefore decided to visit the Middle East, and to experience the 'truth to nature' that he eagerly sought for his religious works. Both Millais and Rossetti were upset at his decision to go but wished him well. Other artists, such as Augustus Egg, warned him that he was in danger of losing his new-found clients if he left. He set off, however, on 13 January 1854, travelling first to Paris and then down to Marseille, where he boarded a ship for Egypt via Malta. In Cairo, he was met by Thomas Seddon (1821–56), a landscape artist who had agreed to go on ahead of him to make arrangements. Hunt made a number of trips including a visit to the Pyramids, persuading a young local woman to model for him. The resulting picture

Above right: WH Hunt, The Afterglow in Egypt, *oil on canvas, 1854.*

THE SCAPEGOAT

At the end of his first year in the Holy Land, and with Seddon now en route back to England, Hunt wrote to Millais about a new painting project he had in mind, depicting the scapegoat in the wilderness as described in the Old Testament. Hunt purchased a goat for this purpose and went into the wilderness with a group of people who also wished to see this barren landscape. Staying under canvas at night and subjecting himself to intense heat, storms and the threat of attack, Hunt nevertheless wrote of the experience as 'a journey of inconceivable delights'.

Above: WH Hunt, Christ Among the Doctors, *gouache, 1887.*

was *The Afterglow in Egypt*. Eventually, Hunt pressed on to Syria before reaching Jerusalem, his final destination. From here he was able to visit a number of locales, including the Mount of Olives and a pilgrimage to Bethlehem.

THE HANNA HADOUB AFFAIR

Hunt was critical of the over-zealous Christian missionaries in Jerusalem, believing that their attempts at conversion of the heathens had nothing to do with religion. He had the courage to speak out against the head of the Anglican community there, Bishop Gobat, who was corrupt. One of the most shocking examples of his corruption was the case of Hanna Hadoub, who had made a fortune and was excommunicated for living off the immoral earnings of his mother, sisters and wife. Gobat not only allowed Hadoub back into the church but also helped arrange the marriage to his second wife who he knew to be a prostitute. Hunt spoke out on behalf of the Christian community and was forced to substantiate his claims.

Right: WH Hunt, Self-portrait, *oil on canvas, 1875.*

His 42-page document of the whole affair was finally published in London in March 1858, outlining not only Gobat's corruption but the complicity of the missionaries as well. After this, Hunt was disillusioned with evangelical religion, preferring instead the inner sanctity of his personal faith.

AFTER THE HOLY LAND

Holman Hunt returned from the Holy Land in financial difficulty, compounded by the fact that he struggled to find buyers for his new paintings. This was also a difficult time in his personal life, and he was forced to break off his engagement to Annie Miller soon after his return, though their relationship continued.

Above: Val Prinsep, Woman Reclining with a Parrot, *oil on canvas, date*

Below: WH Hunt, The Festival of St Swithuns, *oil on canvas, 1866–75.*

Hunt left Jerusalem in October 1855 and did not arrive back in London until the following February. During Hunt's absence, his father had been taken very ill, and he was to die later in the year. While Hunt had been away, his sister Emily had attended art school and was making progress. Their father, who had seen the relative success of his son's career, made Hunt promise to help her in the event of his death, to which he reluctantly agreed. Hunt was also able to resume his relationship with Annie.

ANNIE MILLER

Before leaving for the Holy Land, Hunt had hoped to find a wife to accompany him, but had failed, despite the help of his mother and Millais' wife Effie. He had, however, begun his long relationship with Annie Miller, his beautiful but uncouth model. He decided to put her in the charge of Fred Stephens, a fellow member of the Pre-Raphaelite Brotherhood, while he was away. He planned for Stephens to educate her and make her acceptable in society, so

that he could marry her on his return. Having secured payment for his paintings from Thomas Combe before he left, he gave Stephens £200 for Annie's education. Stephens borrowed some of the money himself, which he did not repay, and Annie's education was less than complete. In fact she had become mistress to both Lord Ranelagh and Rossetti. Hunt's on/off relationship with Annie continued until 1865, when he finally married. Unknown to Hunt, she had married Lord Ranelagh's cousin, only to be rejected later when she became pregnant. She had been paid off by Lord Ranelagh, but also tried in vain to extort money from Hunt in exchange for his letters to her, once she had heard of his marriage.

FINANCIAL MATTERS

Hunt returned from the Holy Land in financial difficulties. He had brought several pictures back but they were as yet unsold. Despite sending *The Scapegoat* back to England, his patron,

Above: WH Hunt, The Lady of Shalott, *illustration, 1857.*

Thomas Combe, who was looking after his business interests, was unable to find a buyer. The work appeared in the 1856 Academy Exhibition to a mixed reception but was eventually sold to Benjamin Windus (1790–1867), an important collector of Turner's work, for the asking price of 450 guineas (about £30,000 today). After the exhibition, Hunt, on the advice of Thomas Combe, applied again for Associateship of the Academy. He was rejected and vowed never to apply again, such was his shame at getting just one vote in support of his application. This humiliation was compounded by the fact that his rejection from the Academy also affected the desirability of his pictures. Like Millais and Rossetti, Hunt was asked to contribute to the Moxon Tennyson, providing some income, but he needed new patrons. At the time of selling *The Scapegoat*, Hunt

had also sold the reproduction rights of *The Light of the World* to the publisher and art dealer Ernest Gambart.

GAMBART

While Hunt was in the Holy Land he began one of his most important pictures, *The Finding of the Saviour in the Temple*. The picture took six years to complete, using Jewish sitters that he encountered in London, continuing his decision to use only Semites when in Jerusalem to attain authenticity in his painting. The picture was sold to Gambart for the princely sum of £5,500 (about £300,000 today), to be paid in instalments. At this date this was the highest price ever paid in England for a single work of art. Hunt decided, probably as a retort for his earlier

rejection, not to exhibit the painting at the Royal Academy. He sold the publishing rights to Gambart as well, and the picture was made more famous through its reproduction as an engraving than it might have been from exposure at the Academy. Like many of Hunt's earlier pictures, it is full of symbolism, containing not only the narrative of the moment but also foretelling Jesus's fate.

PORTRAITURE

Perhaps as a result of seeing Millais' success, Hunt decided to try portraiture shortly after completing *The Finding of the Saviour in the Temple*. Although he was now financially stable, at least in the short term, he needed to be able to have a regular income to marry and raise a family. The founding of the National Portrait Gallery in London in 1856 fuelled his interest, as did his association with the Holland Park circle of artists, who included Leighton and Val Prinsep (1838–1904).

Below: George Boyce, Portrait of Annie Miller, *pencil, 1854.*

RESTLESS TO RETURN

This period was notable for the International Exhibition at which Hunt exhibited in 1862. Soon after his return, Hunt became eager to revisit the Holy Land, but first wanted a wife to accompany him. He married Fanny Waugh in 1865, and the couple set off for the Holy Land the following year.

Hunt's desire for companionship led him to delay his return to the Holy Land until he was married. This break in his travels allowed him to exhibit at London's International Exhibition, which opened in 1862.

THE SEARCH FOR A WIFE

By the early1860s, Hunt had proposed to at least two eligible ladies who declined because of the arduous journey. They included Julia Jackson (1846–95), who was later to marry Leslie Stephen (1832–1904) and have two daughters, who became Vanessa Bell (1879–1961) and Virginia Woolf (1882–1941). It was at this time that Hunt went to stay with Richard Monckton Milnes (1809–95) in Yorkshire. Milnes was a politician and a poet, a member of the Apostles Club alongside Tennyson and others of their era. Hunt stayed in Yorkshire for several weeks, rubbing shoulders with Ford Madox Brown, the writer Wilkie Collins, the poet Swinburne and Richard Burton (1821–90), the explorer and translator into English of *The Arabian Nights*. Many of the guests belonged to the Hogarth Club, a short-lived exhibiting society founded by Hunt and others in defiance of the Royal Academy. In September 1864, Hunt acted as best man at the wedding of one of the Brotherhood, Thomas Woolner to Alice Waugh, the daughter of Dr George Waugh, a wealthy chemist. Afterward, Hunt proposed to Alice's sister Fanny (who had been courted by Woolner for two years but had rejected him), and they were married in December 1865 in London, with Combe and William Rossetti acting as witnesses. Fanny was the model for the face in *Il Dolce Far Niente*, originally modelled by Annie, but not completed.

Right: WH Hunt, Portrait of Fanny Holman Hunt, *oil on canvas, 1866–8.*

THE INTERNATIONAL EXHIBITION

The Great Exhibition of 1851 in London had been a roaring success, making a profit in excess of £186,000 (equivalent today to £16 million). Much of that profit was used to found the Victoria and Albert Museum, the Science Museum and the Natural History Museum, and to establish a school of design. The French responded with the Exposition Universelle, held in Paris in 1855. Although financially it was a disaster, they had included an exhibition of fine and applied arts to demonstrate their position as the European masters in those disciplines. Millais had shown his work *The Order of Release*, which won a silver medal at this exhibition. Watching events across the Channel very carefully, the British replied by staging another

Above: ES Cole, International Exhibition, 1862: Official Opening, *medium unknown, date unknown.*

Above: English School, Portrait of Wilkie Collins, *engraving, date unknown.*

exhibition to be opened in 1862, this time to include fine art. The picture gallery was over 300m (1,000 ft) long, and used natural lighting to help avoid glare. Each nation represented selected a 'father' of their painting tradition, the British using William Hogarth, and showing a range of painters that included Thomas Gainsborough (1727–88), David Wilkie (1785–1841) and John Constable (1775–1837), as well as Sir Joshua Reynolds (1723–92). The Pre-Raphaelite artists represented contemporary British painting. The exhibition preparations were, however, marred by the death of the Queen's Consort Prince Albert in December 1861, and there was a shadow of sadness that cast a shadow over the event.

and continued to wear black for the rest of her long life. The mood in society was somewhat lightened by the preparations for the forthcoming marriage of the Queen's eldest son, Edward, Prince of

Wales (1841–1910), in 1863. Hunt decided on a suitable picture for the occasion, which he continued to work on until 1866 when he finally left again for the Holy Land.

TWO PRINCES

Queen Victoria's consort was Prince Albert of Saxe-Coburg. They were married in 1840 and had nine children. He had been instrumental in establishing, and making a success of, the Great Exhibition of 1851. He almost certainly would have been involved in the creation of the 1862 exhibition, had he not been ill at the time it was announced by the Queen in early 1861. During that year Albert's health deteriorated, and he died of typhoid fever at the age of 42. The Queen never recovered from her loss

Right: W Thomas, Queen Victoria and Prince Albert, *engraving, 1855.*

TO THE EAST AGAIN

Holman Hunt and his new bride began their journey to the Holy Land despite the fact Fanny was pregnant. The couple chose to stall their trip in Italy until afte the baby was born, but a tragic incident brought an end to Hunt's plans and forced a return to England sooner than he ever could have imagined.

At the time of Hunt's departure for the Holy Land in August 1866, Fanny was pregnant, but she accompanied him as planned, despite her family's concerns. Their worries were proven well-founded, as tragedy soon struck the new family.

Above: WH Hunt, Distant View of Nazareth, *watercolour, 1860–1.*

Below: WH Hunt, London Bridge on the Night of the Marriage of the Prince and Princess of Wales, *oil on canvas, 1863–6.*

ITALY

When the newlyweds reached Marseille, they found that they could not take the ship to Alexandria due to an outbreak of cholera. Hunt decided instead to cross the Alps and travel down through Italy, intending to take a ship from Malta instead. They discovered later that the embargo had been extended to all Italian ports. It was decided that they should remain in Florence until after Fanny's confinement. In October, she gave birth to a son, Cyril Benoni, after a difficult labour. Unfortunately, Fanny died from a fever less than two months later. Hunt was inconsolable and even the presence of his friend Woolner, who had come out to Florence to comfort him, had little effect on his grief.

The Waugh family suggested that the child be sent back to England to be cared for by them. Hunt, however, decided to keep him in Italy while he remained there himself. Cyril was to be looked after by Hunt's friends the Spencer Stanhopes, who lived in Florence. Hunt stayed in Italy until September 1867 before returning to England.

ENGLAND

Mr and Mrs Waugh agreed to look after and raise Cyril while his father continued painting. During his absence in Italy, Millais, with good intentions but without his consent, had put Hunt's name forward for election to the Royal Academy. Hunt was rejected again, and was angry with his friend, feeling that he could continue without such patronage. His faith seemed justified: George Waugh commissioned Hunt to paint a portrait of his youngest daughter Edith, as it was soon to be her 21st birthday. During the sittings, Edith confessed her love for Hunt, and he returned her feelings. When the portrait was finished,

Left: WH Hunt, Cyril Benoni Holman Hunt, *oil on canvas, 1880.*

FLORENCE AND ON

With Cyril in the capable hands of the Waugh family, Hunt left for Florence in July 1868. He took a studio and began painting *Bianca*, modelled by Miss Lydiard, with whom he discussed the possibility of marriage. She apparently did not wish to travel, particularly to the Holy Land, and the relationship ended. Hunt decided to complete the monument he had designed for Fanny, before travelling on to Syria. While he was waiting for the stonemason to complete the monuments he began collecting Old Masters. He was in correspondence with Woolner, who had a good eye for antiques, but Hunt made several major and costly mistakes in attribution. Hunt decided to complete the monument to Fanny himself, as the mason was taking too long. Having completed the task he decided to visit Venice. Purely by chance, he ran into Ruskin while he was there and the two men spent several days in each other's company. In August 1869, Hunt arrived in Jerusalem again and took a lease for three years on a house in the Muslim area of the city. The house needed substantial repairs, and while these were being completed he visited Bethlehem, staying there for several weeks.

Below WH Hunt, Ponte Vecchio, Florence, *oil on canvas, c.1866.*

he inscribed a quote from Shakespeare's *Romeo and Juliet*:

> *But my true love is grown to such*
> *excess I cannot sum up sum of half*
> *my wealth.*

There was, however, nothing that could come of it in England, as it was illegal for a widower to marry his deceased wife's sister. Hunt decided to return to Florence to distance himself from Edith.

CONTROVERSY

Hunt had arrived back in the Holy Land, but missed the companionship of a wife and the camaraderie he had previously shared with other artists. The painting he produced at this time sparked controversy through its representation of Jesus, but it was his personal life that would cause the greatest scandal.

The death of Fanny and the impossibility of persuing a relationship with her sister, Edith, meant that Hunt had returned to Jerusalem alone and forlorn. He threw himself into his work, but struggled to purge himself of his feelings for his dead wife's sister.

ALONE IN JERUSALEM

On moving back to Jerusalem he began work on *The Shadow of Death*. His house was large enough for a family of ten, and as Hunt recalled in a letter to William Bell Scott, he walked 'in dismal dignity about the unfriended rooms'. He attempted to learn Arabic but found it too difficult to communicate with his two servants, and was lonely with no other company. His previous companion Seddon had died after revisiting the Holy Land, and his good friend the artist Augustus Egg (1816–63) had also died while in Algiers. Hunt wrote to Mrs

Below: WH Hunt, The Walls of Jerusalem, *watercolour, 1869.*

Waugh asking her to send Cyril out to join him but she refused. When his picture was finished, Hunt had it shipped back to England ahead of him, returning himself in July 1872. He had difficulties in France due to the Franco-Prussian war, but arrived back in England the following month.

Below: WH Hunt, Study of the Artist's Wife, Edith, *coloured chalk, private collection, date unknown.*

HOME AGAIN

Mrs Waugh brought Hunt's son, Cyril, to Victoria Station, London, to meet him from the boat train on his return to England. He had been away for three years and the boy did not recognize him. Although Cyril continued to stay with the Waughs, Hunt ensured that he took him out every day. Millais was away in Scotland and had agreed to let Hunt use his well-equipped studio in his absence. When *The Shadow of Death* arrived in England, it was sold to Agnew's art dealers in Bond Street in London for £11,000, payable in two instalments. The picture was reproduced as an engraving, which sold in huge numbers despite being considered blasphemous in its representation of Christ by some factions of the church. The upsurge in support for the picture was undoubtedly the approval of Queen Victoria, who commissioned a version of it for Windsor Castle, which was called *The Beloved*.

Above: WH Hunt, Mrs Sarah Wilson, the Artist's Sister, *oil on canvas, date unknown.*

Left: Anon, Edith Holman Hunt, *photograph, date unknown.*

A SECOND MARRIAGE

Edith Waugh had spoken to her family and declared her intention to marry Hunt. The Waughs were outraged. Shortly after this George Waugh died; and his wife blamed Edith, who went to live with Fred and Clare Stephens. Cyril was placed in the care of Hunt's Uncle Hobman, although when he heard of his nephew's intentions he was displeased because of the problems that could ensue from the marriage. Despite reservations, Hunt resolved to marry Edith in Switzerland, where it was legal. In the summer of 1875 Edith travelled there, and Hunt later joined her. A civil ceremony took place in November.

RETURN TO JERUSALEM

Hunt brought his son and new wife to the house he had in Jerusalem, but found it uninhabitable and was forced to find new premises. His painting materials had not arrived from England and he was unable to work. Hunt purchased some inferior linen and began with the materials he had left over in the damaged house. He started a new painting that he had sketched out on his previous visit, *The Triumph of the Innocents,* another biblical story. The inferior linen proved difficult to work with, and he decided to abandon it until he returned to England. Hunt managed to purchase a plot of land, and employed a builder to construct a house and studio. Edith became pregnant, but still accompanied her husband on an expedition to the River Jordan, such was her devotion toward Hunt. On 20 September, Edith gave birth to a girl they named Gladys Mulock.

HAPPINESS AND ANXIETY

Despite the scandal, and rifts with family and friends, that their marriage had caused, Hunt and his new bride were very happy together. They were not impervious to outside influences, however, and their happiness was soon marred by anxiety, illness and the death of close friends and colleagues.

Hunt and Edith were joyously happy together, but this did not diminish the stresses and anxieties that Hunt suffered over his work. Plagued by worries over his inferior canvas, and suffering from illness, the early years of the marriage were not free from troubles.

AN INTERUPTED HONEYMOON
In the early years of the Hunt's marriage Gladys, Edith and William's daughter, was seriously ill twice with an inflamed stomach, while Hunt himself did not enjoy the best of health. A large abscess on his leg crippled him and he was continually worrying about the vulnerability of his large picture on the inferior canvas, which exacerbated his illness. He finally broke down with nervous exhaustion in early 1878. With Edith's care he recovered well enough to return to England by April but only had half a canvas to show for over two years' work.

Above left: WH Hunt, Master Hilary – the Tracer, *oil on canvas, 1886.*

LONDON
On his return, Hunt completed a number of paintings based on his time in the Holy Land, including *The Plain of Esdraelon from the Heights Above Nazareth.* He no longer sent work to the Academy, preferring instead the privately owned galleries, such as the Grosvenor. Hunt's work was shown alongside that of Rossetti and Burne-Jones. He had not, however, resolved the problem of the fragile canvas, despite it being relined in London. He decided to take some time off and visit Paris, where he caught typhoid and nearly died. On his return to London, he was unable to work for the rest of the year. The following year, Hunt and his family moved home closer to their friends Fred and Clara Stephens, and in May, Edith gave birth to a boy, Hilary. In the autumn of 1881 the family

Above: WH Hunt, May Morning on Magdalen College Tower, *oil on canvas, 1888–93.*

moved again to Draycott Lodge, a large Regency house in Fulham, London, that had once belonged to Horace Walpole (1717–97).

THE OLD GUARD
In 1882 Rossetti died, and five years later Hunt unveiled the memorial fountain to him beside the Chelsea Embankment. In the same year, Hunt's Uncle Hobman died, leaving him a bequest of £500. The following year saw the demise of Wilkie Collins, and in 1890 William Bell Scott died, leaving Hunt a generous bequest of £800. Even more generous was Mrs Combe; she died in 1893, leaving Hunt £2,000 and his son Cyril £1,000, enough for him to start out on his own career. At the time she died she owned the largest collection of Hunt's work anywhere. Ford Madox Brown also died in 1893.

THE FINE ART SOCIETY

Another new private gallery to open in London in 1876 was the Fine Art Society. Their approach to living artists was to give them one-person shows, and in 1886 Hunt's work was given such exposure. He had borrowed *The Light of the World* from Keble College, Oxford, and was mortified to see the condition it was now in, spending several weeks working to restore it. The exhibition was well received, with Ruskin writing the catalogue.

arriving in Jerusalem the following March. He worked on *The Miracle of the Sacred Fire*, a painting satirizing the ceremony he had witnessed in Jerusalem, which for him was redolent of the corruption he had seen many years before and anathema to the true Christianity he felt in his own heart. He realized that this would be his last journey to the Holy Land and that his experiences there had been cathartic in respect of his own spiritual journey.

Above: WH Hunt Study for the Head of Valentine, *watercolour, 1880*

Right: WH Hunt, My Son Cyril, *pencil, 1877.*

OXFORD

In 1888, Hunt was awarded an honorary degree at Oxford University and was commissioned to paint *May Morning on Magdalen College Tower*, a depiction of a centuries-old tradition in which the college choir sing the *Hymnus Eucharisticus* from the top of its tower in the early morning of 1 May. The event is followed by revelry in the streets of Oxford. Hunt's son Hilary made a cameo appearance in the picture as one of the choirboys.

FINAL VISIT TO THE MIDDLE EAST

Undaunted by the lack of a buyer for *Triumph of the Innocents*, Hunt decided once again to visit the Holy Land. He set off in the autumn of 1891, finally

HUNT'S FINAL YEARS

Toward the end of his life, Hunt's eyesight deteriorated, making it increasingly difficult for him to paint. He was granted numerous honours at this time and his works were featured in several retrospective exhibitions, in appreciation of his 50-year contribution to British art.

The final years of Hunt's career saw him recieve increasing recognition for the contributions he had made toward British art throughout his lifetime. However, in his eyes the greatest achievement of this period was possibly the recognition of the legality of his marriage to his beloved wife, something for which he had long campaigned.

PORTRAIT OF HUNT

In 1900, William Blake Richmond (1842–1921) was commissioned to paint Hunt's portrait to commemorate 50 years of service to the art world. His many friends had set up a fund to pay for it, and in November Hunt was presented with the picture and Leslie Stephen gave the presentation address. The portrait is one of Richmond's best, carefully detailing the worldliness of the sitter, combining it with the serenity of a Rembrandt.

HOLLAND PARK AND SONNING

Draycott Lodge was compulsorily purchased in 1902 to be turned into a school, and the Hunts moved to a

house in Melbury Road in Holland Park, west London. Edith and the as yet unmarried Gladys furnished their new home. They also wanted a country retreat for the summer, having moved from then-rural Fulham, and Hunt bought some land at Sonning in the Thames Valley for this purpose.

Above: WH Hunt, The Importunate Neighbour, *oil on canvas, 1895.*

THE LIGHT OF THE WORLD

William Butterfield (1814–1900), the architect of Keble College chapel, Oxford, had stated in 1873 that Hunt's *The Light of the World* was too small to be of significance in that location. The artist still felt deeply hurt by this slight years later, and decided to paint a larger version. Due to his failing eyesight, Hunt called on the assistance of Edward Hughes, the nephew of his old friend Arthur. The work was completed in late 1903 and shown in a private viewing at Melbury Road. One of the visitors was Charles Booth (1840–1916), a wealthy ship-owner who purchased the painting for an undisclosed sum. An integral part of the transaction was that it was to tour different parts of the world as a travelling sermon after being on display at the Fine Art Society in London for

Left: Sir Hugh Casson, Keble College, Oxford, *lithograph, 20th century.*

THE DECEASED WIFE'S SISTER'S ACT

Since being married to Edith, Hunt had, with many others, vigorously campaigned about the law against marrying the sister of your deceased wife. Although they had been married legally abroad, it was the non-acceptance of his marriage by the conservative faction in English society that rankled him. Hunt had always felt that painting commissions for high office in church and state had eluded him because of this arcane law, but in 1907 an Act of Parliament was passed that recognized the legality in England of his marriage to Edith.

most of 1904. It is estimated that Booth must have paid Hunt about £1,000 for the picture and spent about £5,000 on the tour around Canada, Australia, New Zealand and South Africa, finally returning it to England in 1907. Originally it had been assumed that the picture would be presented to the Tate Gallery, but the trustees rejected it, possibly at the behest of Booth himself, who perhaps felt that its rightful place as a religious and Protestant icon was in St Paul's Cathedral, where it still resides.

FINAL HONOURS

Aside from his honorary degree at Oxford, King Edward VII awarded Hunt an Order of Merit in 1905. His work was also well represented in an exhibition at the newly founded Whitechapel Art Gallery, and two major

retrospective exhibitions of his paintings were curated in 1906 at the Manchester Art Gallery and at the Leicester Galleries in London. Hunt was unable to paint any longer due to his failing eyesight and decided to write a memoir of his career as an artist. Apart from his own biography he decided to include accounts of the Brotherhood. He produced a two-volume book called, unsurprisingly, *Pre-Raphaelitism and the Pre-Raphaelite Brotherhood*, published in 1905 and dedicated 'To my wife'.

DEATH AND INTERMENT

Hunt died at Melbury Road on 7 September 1910, after spending the summer at Sonning. His funeral was at St Paul's Cathedral, where his ashes were interred in the crypt next to the tomb of fellow Pre-Raphaelite, Millais.

Above: Anon, Caricature of Holman Hunt *for* Vanity Fair, *date unknown.*

Left: Sir William Blake Richmond, Florence Nightingale, *oil on canvas, date unknown.*

ARTISTS ASSOCIATED WITH THE MOVEMENT

There were several eminent Pre-Raphaelite artists in the first and second waves of the Brotherhood. This section deals with some of those who were at the forefront of the movement, including Ford Madox Brown, Edward Burne-Jones and John Waterhouse, among others. However, there were many lesser-known artists who emulated the Pre-Raphaelite style. The contributions of John Ruskin and William Morris, both of whom were closely aligned with, and held influence over, the Pre-Raphaelites are also examined in these chapters, as well as the legacy of the Pre-Raphaelite movement and its ambition to change the face of British art for ever.

Above: Frederick Hollyer, William Morris, Burne-Jones and Families, *photograph, 1874.*
Left: Ford Madox Brown, The Pretty Baa Lambs, *oil on panel, 1852.*

MADOX BROWN'S EARLY YEARS

The young Dante Gabriel Rossetti was heavily influenced by the early works of Ford Madox Brown, and eventually became his studio assistant. It was through this contact with Rossetti that Madox Brown became aware of the Pre-Raphaelite ethos and sought to incorporate it into his own work.

Ford Madox Brown was born, raised and educated on the Continent, a fact that would heavily influence his artistic style throughout his career.

BACKGROUND

Raised and educated mainly in Belgium, Ford Madox Brown was influenced by the Dutch and Spanish Old Masters from an early age, but it was his tutelage under Gustave, Baron Wappers (1803–74), the history painter, that encouraged him to try narrative art. He married in 1840 and moved to London four years later. In 1845–6 he visited Rome, where he saw quattrocento pictures, but he was more impressed by the work of Friedrich Overbeck (1837–1905) and the other German Nazarenes, who employed a simpler pictorial form in their paintings.

Above: Friedrich Overbeck, The Adoration of the Kings, *oil on panel, 1813.*

Left: Ford Madox Brown, The Execution of Mary, Queen of Scots, *oil on canvas, 1840.*

THOMAS CARLYLE

Like many Victorians, Madox Brown was attracted to the writings of Carlyle. Carlyle's book *Past and Present* was published in 1843 and is a critique of the ruling classes in Britain in the 19th century, promoting what he calls an 'aristocracy of talent' to guide the nation out of its poverty. Madox Brown's response is *Work*, a pictorial representation of Carlyle's ideas. The picture depicts Carlyle overseeing a group of labourers, with some artisans wearing bow ties and carrying *The Times* newspaper. The location is Hampstead.

This complex tableau was started and completed in England, with much of the work painted on his visit to Rome in 1845–6. Madox Brown conceived it as a triptych but the ideas for the other panels were later adapted to other paintings, such as *Geoffrey Chaucer Reading the 'Legend of Custance' to Edward III and His Court,* executed in 1851. *The Seeds and Fruits of English Poetry* is an eclectic mix of styles and influences, from the Gothic framework to its reincarnation of early Florentine frescoes and altarpieces. The draughtsmanship is exemplary, as is the perfectly balanced composition. The figures are of great English poets including Shakespeare, Milton, Pope, Byron, Keats and Wordsworth. Madox Brown referred to this work as 'a love offering to my favourite poets'.

ROSSETTI

In March 1848, Rossetti wrote to Madox Brown, praising his work and asking for a job as a studio assistant. Madox Brown saw the letter as sycophantic and impertinent, but was eventually persuaded to take Rossetti on. This arrangement did not last long as the overbearing Madox Brown conflicted with the more temperamental and impetuous Rossetti. Nevertheless, the two remained firm friends and Rossetti acknowledged him as his master, despite the fact that Hunt actually taught him to paint.

PALACE OF WESTMINSTER

On the night of 16 October 1834, the 11th-century Palace of Westminster was ravaged by fire. The Great Hall was the only major part of the buildings to survive. Two years later, and after a large architectural competition, rebuilding began. By the 1840s, further competitions were under way for the interiors; Madox Brown submitted a series of preparatory sketches for paintings but was rejected. One of the successful candidates for the Westminster project was Daniel Maclise (1806–70), who was also influenced by the German Nazarenes, his work *The Spirit of Chivalry* being an exemplar.

TOWARD PRE-RAPHAELITISM

Madox Brown continued developing his style, based on the Nazarene aesthetic, by lightening his palette. The result was *The Seeds and Fruits of English Poetry,* begun in 1845 and completed in 1851, a work that owes much to Maclise.

Above: GE Watts, Portrait of Thomas Carlyle, *oil on canvas, date unknown.*

Below: Ford Madox Brown, The Seeds and Fruits of English Poetry, *oil on canvas, 1845.*

MADOX BROWN CONTRIBUTES

Through his relationship with Rossetti, Ford Madox Brown was soon accepted within the Pre-Raphaelite Brotherhood, and sought to employ their aesthetic sentiments in his own work. His first attempts to emulate the style were received badly, however, and he failed to gain John Ruskin's support.

Tutoring Rossetti brought Madox Brown into the inner sanctum of the Pre-Raphaelites. Probably due to an age difference, Madox Brown did not actually join the Brotherhood, but was heavily influenced by their style and had soon adopted their naturalistic approach in his own paintings.

ASSOCIATION WITH THE PRB

Despite not being a member of the Brotherhood, Ford Madox Brown was highly esteemed by the Pre-Raphaelites and was even asked to contribute to

Below: Ford Madox Brown, The Bromley Family, *oil on canvas, 1844.*

The Germ. The Brothers encouraged him to lighten his palette and he retouched his *Chaucer* picture accordingly; it was well received at the 1851 Academy. Madox Brown became interested in landscape painting and in the minute detail in works by Millais and Hunt. *Pretty Baa Lambs* is a fine example, although it is only small. Madox Brown's first truly Pre-Raphaelite work was a religious painting, *Jesus Washing Peter's Feet,* begun in 1851. The copper bowl in the painting demonstrates the Pre-Raphaelite technique that Brown adopted of painting into a wet and much lighter canvas ground.

Above: Frederick Hollyer, Portrait of Ford Madox Brown, *platinum print, c.1870.*

A NEW WIFE

Madox Brown's first marriage in 1840 was to his cousin Elizabeth Bromley. One of his earliest paintings is *The Bromley Family,* depicting her relatives. One of the reasons Madox Brown visited Rome in 1845 was a hope that the climate would help her tuberculosis. He stayed in Rome until she died the following year, while desperately trying to get home to England. They had a daughter, Lucy, born in 1843, who was later to become an artist and married Michael William Rossetti. In 1848, Madox Brown met Emma Hill and asked her to model. Unlike Elizabeth, she was very seductive but uneducated and from a working-class family. They had a child, Catherine, in 1850 and were eventually married in 1853. Emma appears in several of his pictures, including *The Last of England.*

Right: Ford Madox Brown, The Artist's Wife, Emma, *coloured chalks, 1853.*

STUDIO

Madox Brown's studio was in Stockwell, south London, where he began experimenting with painting *en plein air*, seeking to capture the essence of summer light. Prior to this time his paintings were executed in the studio. *Pretty Baa Lambs* is painted on a bright, white canvas ground and he worked out of doors on this picture for five months, as recorded in his diary. The painting depicts Emma with their new baby Catherine (Katty).

EXHIBITIONS AND PATRONS

Pretty Baa Lambs was exhibited at the 1852 Academy, badly positioned and castigated by the critics. As a result it was unsold and remained so until it was purchased in 1859 by one of Madox Brown's later patrons, James Leathart (1820–95). His other entry in 1852 was *Jesus Washing Peter's Feet*, which was also badly hung, and was criticized mainly for the scantily clad figure of Jesus. The painting was reworked and his efforts were rewarded when he received the £50 prize at the Liverpool Exhibition in 1856. Eventually Madox Brown stopped sending his paintings to the Academy, preferring instead the regional galleries and private patrons.

Below: Ford Madox Brown, Hampstead, a sketch from nature, *watercolour, 1857.*

Despite supporting the other Pre-Raphaelites, he did not have the support of John Ruskin (who referred to one of his landscapes as 'ugly').

Below: Ford Madox Brown, The Bromley Children, *oil on canvas, 1843. This portrays three children of Brown's cousin Augustus Frederick Bromley (1815–1843).*

MADOX BROWN'S LEGACY

Ford Madox Brown started to design furniture and stained glass to boost his income, and was a a founding member of William Morris's firm. At this time he found a new patron in the form of Frederick Leyland, and received a commission to paint a series of murals for Manchester's newly built Town Hall.

Struggling to maintain an income through his painting, Madox Brown was driven to design furniture to boost his finances. This led to an interest in design that he was able to exploit fully as a member of 'The Firm'.

THE FIRM

Brown designed stained glass and furniture for the Firm until, like Rossetti, he was dismissed when Morris restructured the company in 1875. The designs Brown executed influenced his later paintings, which were often on religious themes and became more decorative. An example is *The Entombment* of 1866–8, which is more linear than his earlier paintings and combines the delicate colouring of early Florentine painting with the new Aestheticism of the 1860s. It is probably the latter aspect that most appealed to Brown's patron Frederick Leyland (1831–92).

Below: Ford Madox Brown, The Expulsion of the Danes, *wall mural, c.1880.*

FREDERICK LEYLAND

A wealthy ship-owner based in Liverpool, Frederick Leyland established a lucrative transatlantic steamship business, the Leyland Line. He befriended Rossetti, and through him became an important art patron, initially buying important Italian Renaissance works by, among others, Botticelli and Vasari. Later he patronized contemporary artists such as Rossetti, Burne-Jones, Madox Brown and Whistler. It was Whistler who was commissioned to decorate the dining room at his London residence, 49 Prince's Gate, a scheme that became known as 'The Peacock Room'. The house enabled Leyland to indulge his fantasy of 'living the life of an old Venetian merchant in modern London'.

Right: Ford Madox Brown, The Nativity, *stained glass, date unknown.*

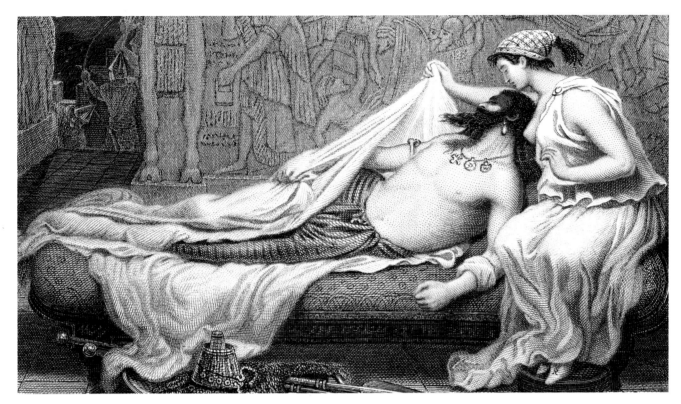

RETROSPECTIVE EXHIBITION

Due to his withdrawal from Academy exhibitions, it was necessary for Madox Brown to market his own work. He did not exhibit in private galleries, but found a succession of patrons such as the banker George Rae (1817–1902), who purchased six of his works, the industrialist James Leathart, and collectors of Pre-Raphaelite paintings such as John Miller. Madox Brown also organized his own retrospective exhibition in 1865 in central London.

MANCHESTER TOWN HALL

In 1878, Madox Brown was commissioned to paint a series of murals for the newly built Manchester Town Hall. There are 12 panels, each of which depict an aspect of Manchester's history, designed to demonstrate the strategic importance of Manchester and its part in the British Empire. The first eight panels were painted directly on to the walls, and the final four are painted on canvas. Madox Brown began the commission in 1879 and completed it just before he died in 1893. He moved to Manchester with his family to execute the work.

Right: Ford Madox Brown, The Entombment, *1866–8.*

Above: Ford Madox Brown, Sardanapalus, *etching, 1869.*

STUDIO ASSISTANTS

Madox Brown had four children, Lucy (1843–94), Catherine (1850–1927), Oliver (1855–74) and Arthur (1856–7). The last of these died in infancy but the others all assisted their father in his studio. Oliver, a promising painter and poet, died when he was just 19, but Lucy and Catherine became artists in their own right.

The renowned watercolour landscape artist Albert Goodwin (1845–1932) also acted as his studio assistant.

LEGACY

More than any other Pre-Raphaelite artist, Madox Brown explored light and its characteristics in his painting, building on one of the tenets of Turner's oeuvre. He was avant garde for his time, predating the Impressionist agenda by at least ten years.

BURNE-JONES'S EARLY YEARS

An accomplished draughtsman, Edward Burne-Jones showed promise as an artist from a young age. Inspired by tales of romantic chivalry, as well as the works of Ruskin and Rossetti, whilst studying at Oxford, he had soon positioned himself to move within the Pre-Raphaelite circle.

Initially destined for the priesthood, Edward Burne-Jones was led by his artistic skill, fuelled by the inspiration he found in the writings of Ruskin and Carlyle, as well as his admiration for Rossetti, to change tack and pursue a career as an artist.

BACKGROUND

Edward Coley Burne-Jones was born in Birmingham on 28 August 1833, his mother dying from complications a few days later. His father was a picture frame-maker whose housekeeper, Ann Sampson, brought up Edward until the age of 11; he was then sent to King Edward's School in the city, already showing the desire and the talent to become an artist. In 1853 he went up to Exeter College, Oxford, to become a priest, and met William Morris who shared the same ambition. Both became disillusioned with the Tractarian movement they had hoped to encounter there, and instead read Ruskin and Carlyle. Both Carlyle and Ruskin were critical of modernity and the adverse effect it was having on the working classes. Burne-Jones responded by declaring his intention of becoming an artist, with a missionary zeal inspired by the medievalism of Oxford.

ROSSETTI

While he was at Oxford, Burne-Jones saw Rossetti's *The First Anniversary of the Death of Beatrice*, finding it 'our greatest wonder and delight'. He subsequently left Oxford without graduating and moved to London in 1856, where he sought out Rossetti, who was delighted to adopt a new protégé. He introduced the young man to his own group, which included John Ruskin, who helped him to win a commission to decorate the Oxford Union. He worked under the guidance of Rossetti and alongside Morris.

Above: JM Ince, Exeter College, Oxford, watercolour, 1835.

Ruskin was to write of this venture: 'They're all the least bit crazy and it is very difficult to manage them', such was the excitement and impetuosity of the group.

DESIGN

From 1856, Burne-Jones and Morris shared lodgings at Red Lion Square in Bloomsbury. They began designing domestic furniture that eschewed the modern aesthetic as exemplified at the Great Exhibition of 1851. One of the finest examples of Burne-Jones' early furniture designs is the panel *The Prioress's Tale*, which he painted for Morris in 1859. He had been asked in 1857 to design some stained glass for a church in Maidstone, Kent, which he completed in 1861. Ruskin was apparently 'driven wild with joy' at seeing the work, which showed a remarkable understanding of the linearity needed for that medium.

Above: Anon, Portrait of Edward Burne-Jones, *photograph, date unknown.*

Above: E Burne-Jones. The Knight's Farewell, *pen and ink on paper, 1858.*

THE WORKING MEN'S COLLEGE

The WMC was set up in 1854 as part of the Christian Socialist movement to provide education and training to working class males. Among the educators were Ruskin, Madox Brown, Rossetti and Burne-Jones, who taught drawing from 1859.

DRAWINGS

In 1858 Burne-Jones began a series of pen and ink drawings with a medieval theme underpinned by the fact they were on vellum. These exquisite drawings combine Rossetti's romantic notions with Ruskin's attention to detail. Burne-Jones' work *The Knight's Farewell,* which is lighter in tone than the vellum drawings, is a fine example of this combination. His later drawings for Morris's poems and illustrations for the Kelmscott Press are among the finest examples of draughtsmanship by any artist of any age.

Georgiana had two children, Philip, born in 1861, and Margaret in 1866. Another child was born in 1864, but died in infancy. The Burne-Joneses continued to live in Bloomsbury.

FAMILY

Burne-Jones had courted Georgiana MacDonald since 1855, and married her in 1860. They were married on 9 June, the same day as the supposed death of the poet Dante's Beatrice. This would not have been a coincidence, as Burne-Jones was still under the influence of Rossetti. Burne-Jones and

Right: E Burne-Jones and Philip Webb, The Prioress's Tale, *painted wardrobe, 1859.*

BURNE-JONES DEVELOPS

'The Firm' was founded in 1861, with Burne-Jones as one of the founding members. During this time he became especially well known for his stained glass designs, and his painting style continued to develop, sparking the interest of several wealthy patrons. He also embarked on an affair with Maria Zambaco.

William Morris and Burne-Jones founded 'The Firm' in 1861, with Rossetti and Madox Brown. This marked a period of heightened creativity for Burne-Jones, and he received increasing exposure for his work. He did experience some criticism for his depictions of full-frontal male nudity, however, leading him to withdraw from exhibiting publicly for several years. Luckily, events in his private life brought him into contact with wealthy patrons and he was able to sustain himself as an artist.

'THE FIRM'

Burne-Jones was a founding member of Morris, Marshall, Faulkner & Company under the direction of William Morris. His designs for stained glass are among the finest of the period. Although he ceased to be a partner when 'The Firm' was restructured in 1875, he was retained as the sole designer for stained glass. He also designed some very fine tapestries and produced evocative graphics for Kelmscott Press in the 1890s, most notably for *The Works of Geoffrey Chaucer*, published in 1896.

Below: E Burne-Jones Maria Zambaco, *pencil, c.1868.*

Left: Frederick Hollyer, William Morris, Burne-Jones and Families, *photograph, 1874.*

ITALY

In the summer of 1862, Burne-Jones visited Italy in the company of Ruskin. Ruskin's *Stones of Venice*, published in 1851–3, commended the beauties of Venetian architecture with the 'pleasure' taken by its masons in creating it. Ruskin paid for the trip in exchange for Burne-Jones copying some of the Old Masters of the Italian Renaissance. Although these copies appeared laborious to the young artist, the influence they had on his painting is obvious, for example in *Cupid and Psyche* (1865). It is quite clear, if one compares this to *Merlin and Nimue* (1861), that Ruskin's influence is directing Burne-Jones away from medievalism and toward a new aesthetic.

Above: GF Watts, Portrait of Edward Burne-Jones, *oil on canvas, 1870.*

Above: E Burne-Jones, Angels Climbing and Descending, *stained glass, date unknown.*

THE SOCIETY OF PAINTERS IN WATERCOLOUR

Burne-Jones was elected an Associate of the Society of Painters in Watercolour (later the Old Watercolour Society and then, the Royal Watercolour Society) in 1864. Watercolours were always badly hung at the Academy, a symptom of the heavy bias toward oils, which led to the setting up of this dedicated Society in 1804. In 1870, Burne-Jones resigned as a member of the Society in response to criticism he received for the full frontal male nudity in his work *Phyllis and Demophoön*. This led to a period of depression for Burne-Jones; he withdrew from public exhibitions for several years, and his painting style was affected.

KENSINGTON AND NEW PATRONS

In 1865, Burne-Jones and his family moved to Kensington Square, an affluent area of London where many leading artists lived. He was also brought into contact with their patrons, including Frederick Leyland and William Graham. Graham was a wealthy merchant and collector of Pre-Raphaelite paintings. He did not use an agent, did not believe in intellectual connoisseurship, and only purchased works that he personally liked. His relationship with Burne-Jones began in 1861 with the purchase of *Laus Veneris*. He continued to buy his works until the artist's death in 1885, referring to him as a 'genius for his perception and instinct in painting'. Burne-Jones remained in Kensington for two years before settling at The Grange in Fulham.

MARIA ZAMBACO

The model for the clinging female figure in *Phyllis and Demophoön* was Maria Zambaco, the niece of the wealthy art patron Alexander Ionides (1810–90). When her father died, she inherited a fortune and, in 1861, she married Demetrius Zambaco, a Parisian doctor, from whom she separated in 1866. Returning to London she took a fervent interest in art, eventually becoming an accomplished sculptor. In the interim she modelled for Burne-Jones, and became his mistress. It was a very passionate and physical affair, conducted between 1868 and 1870. The artist tried several times to end the relationship but Zambaco threatened to kill herself with laudanum, a threat he probably took seriously in view of Lizzie Siddal's fate. The scenario is played out to great effect in *Phyllis*.

BURNE-JONES FINDS SUCCESS

The critical backlash that Burne-Jones had received, combined with the aftermath of his tumultuous affair with Maria Zambaco, drove him into a state of depression. This period of self-doubt was eased by a second visit to Italy, and the period after his return was one of great recognition for the artist.

There had been a noticeable change in Burne-Jones's paintings when he returned from his visit to Venice with Ruskin in 1862, and his second visit to Italy marked another change in style for the artist. His subsequent works were on a grander scale, and he switched from watercolours to oils. This change was well received by critics and heralded the resurgence of Burne-Jones as an important and highly respected figure.

ITALY AGAIN

In 1871, Burne-Jones decided to visit Italy again as a result of the depression that had overwhelmed him in the wake of the Zambaco affair and the Watercolour Society debacle. He felt that his work had been seen as too eccentric and needed to be slightly more mainstream. Visiting Rome for the first time, he lay on his back for hours staring at Michelangelo's Sistine Chapel ceiling. He also studied other artists of the period such as Botticelli and Piero della Francesca, whose work 'made him feel alive again'. On his return to England, Burne-Jones moved away from watercolour as his main medium to oils in order to paint on a grander scale. He took on a studio assistant, Thomas Rooke, who remained until Burne-Jones's death in 1898. He also began to paint in series format, such as the 'Pygmalion' series of 1875–8, which truly demonstrated his artistic versatility.

SUBSEQUENT WORKS

From 1876 to 1880, Burne-Jones worked on *The Golden Stairs*, a large-scale, complex work that evokes mood rather than a narrative. It shows skilled, detailed draughtsmanship, and has elements of archaism as well as an air of modernity

Right: TM Rook, Interior of the Home of Edward Burne-Jones, *watercolour, date unknown.*

that influenced subsequent admirers of his work, such as Picasso. Another painting he was working on at the time was *The Mill*, not completed until 1882, which was anti-modernist, in line with Ruskin's rejection of the machine in favour of natural sources of power. It was, however, a romantic notion: an aspect that Burne-Jones never lost in his work. These paintings seem to combine aspects of early Italian and Dutch Renaissance influences, with Burne-Jones having confessed he had wanted to 'do a painting like Van Eyck'.

RECOGNITION

In 1880, Burne-Jones purchased a house in Rottingdean on the Sussex coast, wanting a quieter and more private life for part of each year. The following year he was given an honorary degree from Oxford University for his contribution to British art, and in 1883 both he and William Morris were given honorary fellowships at Exeter College, their alma mater. There was however a rift between the two men in that Morris was using his art for political purposes, helping to found the Social Democratic

Left: Frederick Hollyer, Memorial Exhibition of Edward Burne-Jones, photograph, 1898.

their exhibitions and resigned in 1893. At the time of his election he was one of the most important artists in Britain. He continued to show work, mainly at the Grosvenor Gallery and its successor, the New Gallery, and praise was still heaped upon him. At the 1889 Exposition Universelle in Paris, famed for the opening of the Eiffel Tower, Burne-Jones showed *King Cophetua and the Beggar Maid*, another large-scale painting that one critic referred to as 'the exhibition of the soul'. The artist was awarded the Légion d'Honneur, and possibly in response to this, the outgoing Prime Minister William Gladstone created Burne-Jones a baronet in 1894. Burne Jones died on 17 June, 1898. A memorial service was held for him six days later in Westminster Abbey,

WHISTLER VS RUSKIN

Burne-Jones's 'Pygmalion' series were exhibited at the Grosvenor Gallery in 1879. He had shown works there already at the two previous years' exhibitions. The opening exhibition of 1877 had precipitated one of the most infamous cases in art history. Ruskin visited the exhibition and saw Whistler's painting *Nocturne in Black and Gold: The Falling Rocket*. He subsequently wrote

I have seen, and heard, much of Cockney impudence before now; but never expected to hear a coxcomb ask two hundred guineas for flinging a pot of paint in the public's face.

Whistler subsequently sued Ruskin for libel, winning his case but awarded the derisory sum of one farthing. Burne-Jones was called to give evidence on Ruskin's behalf. What Ruskin objected to was the supposed lack of finish in the painting. Although he won, Whistler was made bankrupt and Ruskin lost credibility as an art critic. The trial would be brought up in debates well into the 20th century about the purpose and meaning of art.

Fund, a Marxist radical group established in 1881. In contrast, Burne-Jones believed in the spiritual and contemplative value of art. He was rewarded for his apparent conservatism by the Royal Academy, who elected him an Associate Member in 1885. However, he only showed one work at

Right: E. Poynter, Portrait of Georgiana Burne-Jones, oil on canvas, 1870.

JOHN WATERHOUSE

A latecomer to the movement, John Waterhouse first embraced Pre-Raphaelitism several decades after the dissolution of the Brotherhood, combining the group's aesthetic with his own interest in classical themes. His style was critically acclaimed and he was soon elected as an Associate of the Royal Academy.

John William Waterhouse (1849–1917) was a relative latecomer to Pre-Raphaelitism, being born in the same year that the Brotherhood exhibited their works for the first time as the PRB. His parents were both artists, and his father, William (bap. 1816, d. 1890), lived and worked in Kensington from 1854. He was one of four children, two of whom were to die of tuberculosis before 1860, as did their mother.

EDUCATION AND EARLY CAREER

At school, Waterhouse enjoyed history but entered the Royal Academy Schools to study sculpture in 1870, and soon began to exhibit paintings in private galleries such as the Dudley. Early influences tended to be the more contemporary classical artists, such as Leighton and Lawrence Alma-Tadema, before he finally developed his own particular style, infusing the classical with the later Pre-Raphaelitism of Rossetti and Burne-Jones. His painting *Sleep and His Half Brother Death* combined his love of Roman history with a saleable narrative that made it suitable for his first Academy Exhibition picture, shown in 1874. His subsequent paintings were critically successful and attracted the attention of a patron, Sir John Aird (1833–1911).

MARRIAGE AND LATER CAREER

In 1883, Waterhouse married the artist Esther Kenworthy (1857–1944), and they lived together in St John's Wood, north London, close to other artists of their generation. It was at this time that Waterhouse developed a penchant for

Above right: JW Waterhouse, A Study for The Boreas, *red chalk, 1903.*

Right: JW Waterhouse, Visit of a Sick Child to the Temple of Aesculapius, *oil on canvas, 1877.*

Above: JW Waterhouse, Spring, *watercolour, 1900.*

depicting the tragic female and the *femme fatale*, as seen in *Hylas and the Nymphs*. His most famous painting, *The Lady of Shalott* (1888), was possibly inspired by seeing Millais' exhibition two years before at the Grosvenor Gallery. Waterhouse was also interested in painting the occult, again depicting woman as an enchantress, as seen in *The Magic Circle* (1886), which also has Middle Eastern influences. It was shown at the 1886 Academy Exhibition, described by one critic as 'original in conception and pictorial in its results'.

THE ROYAL ACADEMY

Waterhouse was elected an Associate of the Royal Academy in 1885, and worked as a tutor in the Life and Painting Schools from 1887, before becoming a full Academician in 1895. In the 1890s Waterhouse continued the theme of heroines and enchantresses to great acclaim. His *Ulysses and the Sirens* of 1891 was praised at the Academy as 'a considerable advance upon all his antecedent work'. It was purchased at the time by the National Gallery of Victoria in Melbourne, Australia, only the second of his paintings to be acquired for a public gallery. It was recommended by the Academy's president, Sir Frederic Leighton.

Aside from mythical subjects, Waterhouse also continued to paint literary characters popular with the Pre-Raphaelites, such as Keats's *La Belle Dame Sans Merci*, Shakespeare's Juliet and Tennyson's Mariana.

TEACHING

The artist took students on for art training in his large house. He was also a tutor at the nearby St John's Wood Art School and the King's College School of Art for Women. However, little correspondence from or to him survives, suggesting he was a very private person. He had no children and appears to have had a very conservative lifestyle.

PATRONS AND PORTRAITS

Waterhouse enjoyed the patronage of several art collectors, including George McCulloch (1848–1907), a mine owner who purchased several Pre-Raphaelite paintings, such as Millais' *Sir Isumbras…* and *The Wedding of Psyche* by Burne-Jones. Waterhouse also gained the patronage of the financier Alexander Henderson (1850–1934), later first Baron Faringdon, who owned over 30 paintings by him. As well as his narrative pictures, Waterhouse painted portraits in his later years, mainly landscape, such as *Spring*. Like Rossetti's, they embody the artist's vision of the ideal beauty.

Below: JW Waterhouse, Portrait of the Artist's Wife, *oil on canvas, date unknown.*

COLLINS AND HUGHES

Both Charles Collins and Arthur Hughes sought to emulate the Pre-Raphaelite style, and produced works that were heavily influenced by Millais. Neither artist became a full member of the Brotherhood however, with Charles Collins being refused membership on aesthetic grounds.

As well as the official members of the Pre-Raphaelite Brotherhood, there were many artists who were closely associated with the group and adhered to their style and ethos. Charles Collins and Arthur Hughes were both early supporters of the Pre-Raphaelite cause.

CHARLES COLLINS
The father of Charles Allston Collins (1828–73) was a painter and member of the Royal Academy, and his eldest brother was the novelist Wilkie Collins, who wrote *The Woman in White*. Charles was proposed by Millais for the Pre-Raphaelite Brotherhood, but Woolner rejected him on aesthetic grounds, somewhat unfairly given that he had not produced anything of note that could be described as Pre-Raphaelite.

Religion, particularly Tractarianism, attracted Collins both spiritually and as a subject matter. Many of his paintings have a religious theme, most notably *Convent Thoughts,* begun in 1850 when he was staying with Millais at Oxford. It was here that he met Thomas Combe, who was later to buy the picture after Millais recommended his patron to purchase it at the 1851 Academy Exhibition. It has been suggested that he purchased the painting as a companion piece to Millais' *The Return of the Dove to the Ark,* which he already owned, and which was also shown at the Academy in the same year. *Convent Thoughts* reflects not only Millais' influence but also the fidelity to nature advocated by Ruskin.

MARRIAGE
In 1860, Charles Collins married Kate Dickens (1839–1929), the second daughter of the writer Charles Dickens, a personal friend of Wilkie Collins. Like his brother, Charles also became a writer after abandoning painting in the late 1850s. His most successful work was a collection of witty essays entitled *The Eye-Witness,* published in 1860. His last artistic works were the illustrations for Dickens' unfinished novel *The Mystery of Edwin Drood,* which was being serialized up until his death in 1870. Charles died from cancer three years later.

ARTHUR HUGHES
The youngest of all the early Pre-Raphaelites, Arthur Hughes (1832–1915) exhibited his first painting, *Musidora Bathing,* at the Academy in 1849 aged just 17. It already showed Pre-Raphaelite tendencies in its subject matter, and after reading *The Germ* he became interested in Pre-Raphaelitism. His first work in this style was *Ophelia,* which used the same subject as Millais' painting of the same name. Hughes did not actually meet Millais until the day

Left: Arthur Hughes, Home from Market from 'Leisure Hour', *engraving, 1888.*

Top: Charles Collins, Study for 'Convent Thoughts', *watercolour and gouache, 1851.*

Above left: Charles Dodgson, Arthur Hughes and his Daughter, *photograph, date unknown.*

Above: Charles Allston Collins, Portrait of Wilkie Collins, *oil on canvas, 1853.*

before the Academy Exhibition of 1852 when both pictures were shown. In 1855, Hughes used a similar subject to Holman Hunt's *Eve of St Agnes* of 1848, but this later picture differs in structure and content. It was shown at the Academy in 1856, Ruskin declaring that the 'face of the awakening Madeline is exquisite'. At the same exhibition, Hughes also showed *April Love*, generally accepted as his masterpiece of Pre-Raphaelitism. The catalogue of the exhibition contained a quotation from Tennyson's poem *The Miller's Daughter*, to accompany the picture. The painting uses the Ruskinian ideals of natural forms, most notably in the ivy, which symbolizes

everlasting life, and roses; symbols of love. The composition is clearly redolent of Millais' *A Huguenot…* (1851–2). Just prior to executing *April Love*, Hughes married 'his early and only love', Tryphena Foord, who modelled for the picture. The male model was the sculptor Alexander Munro, with whom Hughes shared a studio. Hughes's marriage to Tryphena followed a five-year engagement, which the artist used as a motif in *The Long Engagement*. The painting was begun in 1854 with a different subject matter. Given Hughes's own experience, it seems that he changed his mind during the creation of the painting, which was not completed until 1859.

OXFORD MURALS AND AFTER

Hughes took part in the Oxford murals venture in 1857 alongside Rossetti, who later became a major influence on his work, as seen in *The Brave Geraint*. After he married Tryphena, the couple moved out of London, away from his Pre-Raphaelite colleagues, and had five children. His later pictures are a combination of medieval scenes of chivalry *à la* Rossetti or romantic genre pictures that include children. His later career was spent mainly on illustration work for magazines and books, including producing illustrations to accompany Christina Rossetti's poems.

RUSKIN AND MORRIS

Both John Ruskin and William Morris were close friends and supporters of the Pre-Raphaelite Brotherhood. Ruskin's *Modern Painters* had helped to shape the Pre-Raphaelite ethos, and he had adopted both Millais and Rossetti as protégés. Morris's 'Firm' employed the Brothers as 'Fine Art Workmen'.

Although 15 years in age separated Ruskin and Morris, they shared an idealized vision of how society should function. Both were appalled at the quality of machine-made goods, and the resultant alienation of man-made work, or as Karl Marx later put it 'the relations of production'. The two men envisioned a society in which artisans once more 'enjoyed' their work as they had supposedly done in a previous age.

JOHN RUSKIN: LIFE UNTIL 1849

Ruskin was the only child of a successful wine merchant. He travelled with his parents around Britain and across the Continent, becoming an accomplished poet and sketching in detail everything that excited his imagination. He loved nature and architecture, writing about and sketching both. He managed to combine the two at only 15 years old, writing a series of articles called *The Poetry of Architecture* for Loudon's *Architectural Magazine*. Between 1837 and 1840, Ruskin went up to Oxford University where he won a prize for his poetry, but left with only a minor degree. His first major work was *Modern Painters*, published anonymously in 1843, in which he defended one of England's greatest landscape artists, JMW Turner, from the increasing criticism that he was being subjected to in the press. Ruskin's support of Turner's paintings led him to a career as a critic, and he became the most influential writer on art and architecture in the 19th century. In 1848 he married Effie Gray, a disastrous marriage that was never consummated. Effie was later to leave Ruskin in favour of his protégé Millais.

Above: John Ruskin, Gweiss Rock at Glenfinlas, *pencil and watercolour, 1853–4.*

RUSKIN AFTER 1849

Ruskin was responsible for promulgating Gothic architecture in his most famous books, *The Seven Lamps of Architecture* (1849) and *The Stones of Venice* (1851–3), advocating a 'truth to materials'. Ruskin also came to the rescue of the Pre-Raphaelite Brotherhood in a strongly worded letter to *The Times* and subsequently in his pamphlet *Pre-Raphaelitism*. He continued to support individual artists, particularly Rossetti.

Above: Frederick Hollyer, Portrait of William Morris, *photograph, 1884.*

Above: Andrea Lucchesi, Medallion of John Ruskin, *plaster, date unknown.*

With Rossetti, Morris took a lease on a house in Oxfordshire, Kelmscott Manor. In 1871 he visited Iceland; his spiritual experiences there were reflected in his subsequent writings, most notably the epic poem *Sigurd the Volsung*. Meanwhile, his wife was left behind with Rossetti, and the two became romantically involved.

MORRIS AFTER 1875

Morris restructured the 'Firm' in 1875, calling it simply Morris & Company, giving him full control of its output, and moving the operation to Merton Abbey in Surrey. He diversified the business to include tapestries and woven carpets.

Morris also took a house in Hammersmith, west London, which he named Kelmscott House. In 1877 he set up the *Society for the Protection of Ancient Buildings* in response to the poor quality of the restoration work done in the past, particularly on churches. He eventually left the running of the business to his family, in pursuit of his political agenda for a fairer society, a programme that occupied him fully until his death in 1896.

WILLIAM MORRIS TO 1875

Morris also came from an affluent background, going up to Oxford University in 1853 to study theology and then to be ordained. He was particularly interested in the high Anglicanism of the Tractarians. Disillusioned with the apathy he encountered there, he decided instead to become an artist. His first works were on the Oxford Union project, together with other artists including Burne-Jones and Rossetti. He was also apprenticed to the architectural firm of George Edmund Street, who later designed the Royal Courts of Justice in London, in a Gothic style. Another architect, Philip Webb, who was later to work closely with Morris, was also apprenticed to Street's practice. In 1859, Morris married Jane Burden and moved to the Red House just outside London, designed for them by Webb. Two years later he set up Morris, Marshall, Faulkner & Company, his own firm of 'fine art workmen', thus combining the ideas of artisanship and fine art. The disciplines of architecture, design and fine art were, for him, interrelated, a credo that anticipated European movements in the early 20th century. 'The Firm' took

Right: William Morris, Study for St George's Cabinet, *pen ink and wash, 1861.*

premises in London, with Morris and his family, which now included two daughters, moving there as well in 1865. The company sold furniture and furnishings including wallpapers, tapestries and carpets. Morris's oft quoted maxim was 'Have nothing in your house that you do not know to be useful, or believe to be beautiful', a reaction to the excessive ornament and decoration fashionable at the time.

MINOR PRE-RAPHAELITE ARTISTS

Pre-Raphaelitism represented a challenge to authority and raised awareness of contemporary social issues, inspiring many artists to adopt the style. The following pages look as some of the lesser known artists who contributed to the aesthetic, including the remaining members of the official Brotherhood.

THOMAS WOOLNER

After James Collinson, Woolner was the oldest member of the original Pre-Raphaelite Brotherhood (both were born in 1825), and he was the only sculptor in the group. His early work adopts literary themes, such as his figure of Puck from *A Midsummer Night's Dream*, completed in 1847 and shown to the other Brothers in support of his application for membership.

Much of his subsequent Pre-Raphaelite work is medallions of literary figures, although his marble sculpture of *Constance and Arthur* (1857–62) personifies the aesthetic in sculptural form. He wrote poetry and contributed to *The Germ* in the early days, but became disillusioned with Pre-Raphaelitism and instead went to Australia in 1852 to prospect for gold, returning in 1854 to resume his artistic career. His journey to Australia inspired

Madox Brown's painting The *Last of England*. In 1864 Woolner was married to Alice Waugh, with Holman Hunt acting as best man. A year later, Holman Hunt married Fanny, another of the Waugh sisters. Woolner and Alice turned against Hunt later, when he married another of Alice's sisters, Edith, after Fanny's death. Woolner later became a Royal Academician and received several public sculptural commissions.

FREDERICK SANDYS

Sandys was the son of a painter and educated in Norwich at the newly founded Government School of Design in the city. While there he attracted the attention of his first patron, John Gurney, who commissioned a number of watercolours of birds. He also competed for prize money in London, winning a silver medal for a painting of ducks. His second patron was the Reverend James Bulwer, who was writing *A Topographical History of the County of Norfolk*. In 1851, Sandys moved to London and copied from the antiques in the British Museum, and two years later married Georgina Creed: it was a short-lived union, although they never divorced. Sandys came to prominence when he parodied Millais' *Sir Isumbras* with his own work *A Nightmare* in 1857, although he had exhibited regularly at the Academy since 1851 without much recognition. His most productive period was in the 1860s, when he painted several portraits for wealthy patrons, and also produced a number of Pre-Raphaelite gems beginning with *Mary Magdalene* (1860). It was during this period that he came under the influence of Rossetti, living close by him in Chelsea and enjoying the bohemianism of the circle that included Whistler.

Left: Frederick Sandys, Self-portrait with a Wide-brimmed Hat, *oil on board, 1848.*

Above: Thomas Woolner, Portrait Medallion of Tennyson, *bronze, 1855–6.*

Right: Simeon Solomon, The Painter's Pleasaunce, *watercolour and gouache, 1861.*

SIMEON SOLOMON

Solomon was born in 1840 into an affluent Jewish family in the City of London. He entered the Academy Schools in 1855, coming into contact with artists of his own generation such as Albert Moore. He showed regularly at the Academy until 1872, when he moved away from painting to illustration and poetry in the company of Morris and Algernon Swinburne. His career came to an abrupt end in 1873 when he was tried for homosexual offences, never regaining his good name. He died in penury at the workhouse in 1905.

WILLIAM BELL SCOTT

The oldest of all the Pre-Raphaelites, Scott was born in Edinburgh in 1811. His father was a mason and his eldest brother was a painter. He and his brother were trained at the Trustees Academy in the city. William became interested in poetry and in 1831 his poem In *Memory of PB Shelley* was published in Tait's Edinburgh Magazine. At the time of Queen Victoria's accession to the throne in 1837, Scott moved to London and exhibited his

Right: William Bell Scott, John Ruskin Teaching Louisa Stewart-Mackenzie to Draw, *watercolour, 1857.*

first painting, *The Old English Ballad*, at the British Institution in 1839. In 1842 he exhibited *Chaucer, John of Gaunt and Their Wives* at the Academy. But it was Scott's support and influence on the Rossetti family that was one of his most important contributions to Pre-Raphaelitism, particularly in poetry. He wrote poems for *The Germ*, and advised Christina and William Michael Rossetti on their work. His main painting achievement was in the murals for Wallington Hall in Northumberland. Scott wrote his autobiography, which was published posthumously in 1892; this was effectively the first historical account of Pre-Raphaelitism.

WALTER HOWARD DEVERELL

It is likely that in the event of a new nomination to the Pre-Raphaelite Brotherhood after the resignation of Collinson in 1850, Walter Deverell (1827–54) would have been a first choice. However, by this date the enthusiasm for maintaining the group had waned. It was Deverell who discovered Lizzie Siddal working in a millinery shop, and she appeared first of all as Viola in his *Twelfth Night* of 1849–50. Deverell was born in the United States, where his father held a teaching post, but the family returned to England in 1829. He attended Sass's Academy, where he met Rossetti, and like him then enrolled at the Academy Schools. After leaving he became a teacher at the School of Design in Kensington, and was frequently used as a model for the other Pre-Raphaelites due to his boyish good looks.

His career was cut short, firstly by the death of his father in 1853, and then by his own illness, Bright's Disease, from which he died the next year at the age of only 26.

Above: Walter Deverell, Study for 'Twelfth Night', *pen ink and pencil, 1849.*

Below: WH Fisk, Portrait of Frederic George Stephens, *oil on canvas, date unknown.*

JAMES COLLINSON

Collinson came from a relatively affluent family in Nottingham, the youngest of three children. He was timid in nature, and when he enrolled at the Royal Academy Schools in London he met Rossetti and Hunt, who found him dull company. His first submission to the Academy was a genre painting called *The Charity Boy's Debut* which was well received. This and subsequent paintings mark him out as a painter of both sentimental genre and devotional subjects. He was asked by Rossetti to join the Brotherhood, as he and the others admired his paintings. Although he was initiated into the group, by early 1850 he had converted from High Anglicanism to Catholicism and resigned, stating that he could 'not conscientiously as a Catholic assist in parading the artistic opinions of those who are not'. He not only abandoned the Brotherhood but also terminated his relationship with Christina Rossetti, with whom he had an engagement. He subsequently sold his art materials and entered a Jesuit college to train as a priest in late 1852, leaving some time in 1855 without completing his training. Collinson resumed painting and exhibiting at the Academy, but had no further contact with the Pre-Raphaelites.

acquaintance of Millais and Hunt. He was soon employed as a model for these artists, who admired his bone structure. His was first used in Millais' *Ferdinand Lured by Ariel* (1849), and then later in Madox Brown's *Jesus Washing Peter's Feet* (1856). His own offerings as a painter were relatively weak; his only real contribution was *Mother and Child*, an unfinished canvas executed between 1854 and 1856. Stephens was more successful as a critic, however, becoming the leading writer for *The Athenaeum*, a post that he held until 1901, when he retired. He actively promoted the work of his Brothers and helped later to clarify the Pre-Raphaelite aesthetic. He was also an art teacher at University College, London, and wrote several artistic monographs, including one on Lawrence Alma-Tadema. Above all, he helped to promote contemporary British art, establishing a template for the study of its art history in the following century.

HENRY WALLIS

Famous for one painting above all others, Henry Wallis (1830–1916) completed *The Death of Chatterton* in 1856. The painting depicted the suicide of the 18th-century poet Thomas Chatterton, who was a romantic figure for many impoverished artists of Wallis's day. However, some art historians would cite his subsequent work, *The Stonebreaker*, as his masterpiece. Both are seen as exemplars of Pre-Raphaelitism, the first a romantic scene of tragedy that ensured his reputation and the second a work of heartbreaking social realism, inspired by the extreme poverty suffered by many in Britain. Aside from those two pictures Wallis is not known as a Pre-Raphaelite artist, as his subsequent Academy offerings were mostly genre pictures. In the 1870s he travelled extensively to Italy and Egypt and involved himself in archaeology, becoming a collector of artefacts from Persia (modern-day Iran).

FREDERIC GEORGE STEPHENS

Before his election to the Brotherhood, Stephens was enrolled in the Academy Schools from 1844, making the

Above: Henry Wallis, The Stonebreaker, *oil on canvas, 1857.*

Below: James Collinson, The Charity Boy's Debut, *oil on canvas, 1847.*

THE PRE-RAPHAELITE LEGACY

The unrelenting realism of Pre-Raphaelitism became increasingly unfashionable, and the style had all but died out by the early 20th century. The romance of the aesthetic, and of the artists behind it, has endured however, and in recent years Pre-Raphaelite art has experienced a huge resurgence in popularity.

The arrival of Post-Impressionism in Britain in the early 20th century marked a move away from the Ruskinian ideal of 'truth to nature' that the Pre-Raphaelites strove to represent, and their style quickly went out of fashion. However, in more recent years there has been a surge in the market for Pre-Raphaelite art, with several high-profile exhibitions of the style, proving the enduring appeal of the aesthetic.

CHALLENGE TO THE ACADEMY

In the 19th century, several artists and groups of artists began to challenge the authority of the Royal Academy, firstly JMW Turner and then the Pre-Raphaelites. Both had wanted to move away from the dark *chiaroscuro* conventions by lightening their canvases and palettes. This had the effect of generally lightening the tone of most paintings thereafter. In addition, the Pre-Raphaelites introduced literary subject matter and aimed at fidelity to nature, often showing meticulous attention to detail. The latter technique was first used by Millais, and can also be seen in the work of William Powell Frith (1819–1909) and Charles West Cope (1811–90). Under the direction of Frederic Leighton, the President of the Academy in the last quarter of the century, artists returned to mythological and historical subjects, but still with great detail, a trait that continued into the 1900s.

Below: FC Cowper, La Belle Dame Sans Merci, *oil on canvas, 1926.*

SOCIAL ISSUES

The early Pre-Raphaelites did for the visual arts what Dickens had done for literature, creating an awareness of many of the social issues of the day, such as poverty, 'fallen' women, and inequality. Controversially, they also introduced religious themes in a very contemporary idiom, making the issue seem more relevant to the time. A prime example is Hunt's *The Hireling Shepherd*, in which the viewer is confronted with a flirtatious scene in a beautiful landscape, but the painting is in fact an allegory of the church neglecting its flock, symbolized by the straying sheep.

20TH CENTURY PRE-RAPHAELITISM

There were followers of the Pre-Raphaelite aesthetic well into the 20th century, including for example Frank Cadogan Cowper (1877–1958), who was born only five years before the death of Rossetti. He exhibited mainly at the Academy, eventually becoming a full member. His pictures have little to commend them as individualistic, and borrow heavily from Rossetti and others. Nevertheless, his success demonstrates the enduring popularity of the aesthetic, albeit a very conservative one by the time of Cowper's pictures.

REACTION AGAINST PRE-RAPHAELITISM

JM Whistler had, by the end of the 19th century, led a small group of artists to consider the idea of 'art for art's sake'. By the end of the 20th century, however, some of his adherents, including Walter Sickert (1860–1942), were turning instead to the depiction of urban poverty, with the aim of effecting social change. In the inter-war years there was a violent reaction against Victorian painting, and Pre-Raphaelitism as a symbol of that era. The Bloomsbury Group and their leader, the artist and critic

PRE-RAPHAELITE POPULARITY

Pre-Raphaelite art was still out of fashion in the mid-20th century. The composer Andrew Lloyd Webber (b.1948), however, began to collect it in the 1960s. Considered eccentric at the time, his decision was vindicated in 2003 when the Royal Academy held an exhibition called 'Pre-Raphaelite and Other Masters: The Andrew Lloyd Webber Collection'. This is probably the largest collection of its type in private hands anywhere, and has done much to bring Pre-Raphaelitism back into favour with the art-loving public.

Below: Neal Preston, Andrew Lloyd Webber, *photograph, 1994.*

Above: Harold Gilman, A London Street in the Snow, *oil on canvas, 1917.*

Roger Fry (1866–1934), who became as influential as Ruskin had been, led the counter culture. This new wave had begun with Fry's exhibition in 1910, called 'Manet and the Post-Impressionists', in which he introduced Britain to modern French art. Members of the avant-garde, led by Sickert and his Camden Town Group, reacted to this exhibition by depicting urban scenes with unnatural colour to create mood – a technique also used, in a different context, by Rossetti and Burne-Jones.

Right: JM Whistler, Thames: Nocturne in Blue and Silver, *oil on canvas, 1878.*

THE GALLERY

Part two of this book examines the works of the Pre-Raphaelites in chronological order through five sections. The first section deals with the period of the initial impetus of the venture, which for some was losing ground by the mid 1850s. The second section deals with a new impetus under the direction of Rossetti; the third covers the 1860s when new artists joined the fold; and the fourth section looks at the last great flowering by Burne-Jones during the 1870s that continued to the end of the century, which is covered in the final section.

Left: DG Rossetti, The Lady of Shalott, *watercolour, date unknown. private collection, 25 x 18cm (10 x 7in).*

A NEW AESTHETIC
1847–54

A number of young radical artists became disillusioned with the training of the Royal Academy and decided to cut their own path toward a new aesthetic. There was, however, one artist who had already begun this process, Ford Madox Brown. This section covers the period between 1847 and 1855, the birth of Pre-Raphaelitism, the most radical art movement in England for three centuries.

Above: WH Hunt, Valentine Rescuing Sylvia from Proteus, *oil on canvas, 1851, Birmingham Museum and Art Gallery, UK, 99 x 131cm (39½ x 52½in).*

Left: JE Millais, The Return of the Dove to the Ark, *oil on canvas, 1851, The Ashmolean Museum, Oxford, UK, 88 x 55cm (35¼ x 22in).*

WH Hunt, *Christ and the Two Marys*, oil on canvas, 1847, The Art Gallery of South Australia, Adelaide, Australia, 118 x 94cm (43 x 37½in)

Hunt referred to this picture as *The Resurrection Meeting*, and it was his first major religious painting. He needed to find some palm trees for the background, and located them finally at Kew Gardens. Unable to finish the preparatory drawings of the background at Kew, the sympathetic gardener cut off a twelve-foot branch and allowed Hunt to take it back to his studio. This fidelity to nature came from Hunt's consulting Ruskin's book, *Modern Painters* (1843).

JE Millais, *The Death of Romeo and Juliet*, oil on millboard, 1848, Manchester City Art Gallery, UK, 16 x 27cm (6¼ x 10½in)

This small painting has little to do with the Pre-Raphaelite style, as it uses the old conventions of *chiaroscuro* to produce light and dark areas. However, the use of strong colour suggests that Millais was already beginning to consider a brighter palette, as his first truly Pre-Raphaelite picture *Isabella* was begun in the same year as this one.

Ford Madox Brown, *The First Translation of the Bible: John Wycliffe Reading his Translation of the New Testament to his Protector, John of Gaunt, Duke of Lancaster, in the Presence of Chaucer and Gower, his Retainers*, oil on canvas, 1847–8, Bradford Art Gallery, UK, 120 x 153cm (44 x 57½in)

Madox Brown was working on two large history paintings at the same time, this one and his work on *Chaucer*. In this painting the artist has been fastidious in seeking period authenticity in the work, and referred to contemporary sources on medieval furniture by the architect and designer AWN Pugin, as well as Henry Shaw's texts on gothic and medieval detail.

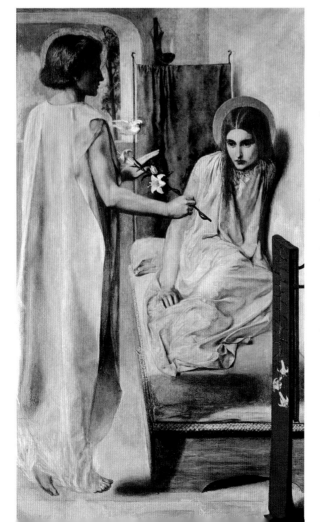

DG Rossetti, *Ecce Ancilla Domini!*, oil on canvas, 1849–50, Tate Gallery, London, UK, 72 x 42cm (28½ x 16¾in)

This extraordinary painting is notable because of Rossetti's use of white robes to denote purity. In conventional paintings of this subject, the Virgin is always depicted in either blue or red garments, and so from this early work it is possible to see the beginnings of Rossetti's desire to use Symbolist ideas, a key feature of his later work. This was the artist's second painting to be exhibited with the suffix PRB appended to his signature.

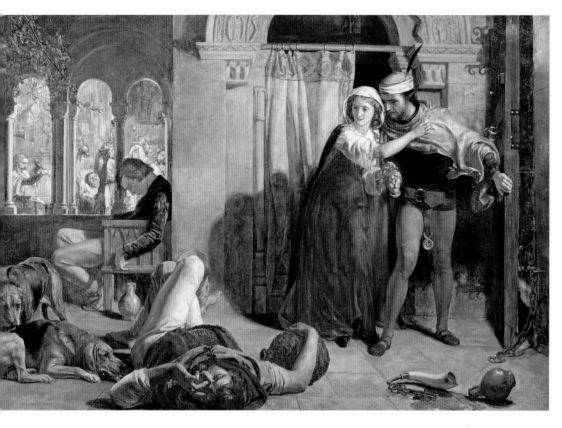

WH Hunt, *The Flight of Madeline and Porphyro During the Drunkenness Attending the Revelry (The Eve of St Agnes),* oil on canvas, 1848, Guildhall Art Gallery, London, UK, 77 x 113cm (30½ x 41in)

In the catalogue for the 1848 Academy, a quotation from Keats' poem *The Eve of St Agnes* was appended to this picture's title to enhance its meaning, hence the subtitle of the work.
At the time of painting, Hunt was studying during the day at the Academy Schools and had to paint the picture by candlelight in Millais' studio, which accounts for the discrepancies in the pictorial shadows.

JE Millais, *Christ in the House of His Parents (The Carpenter's Shop),* oil on canvas, 1849, Tate Gallery, London, UK, 86 x 140cm (34½ x 52in)

This was possibly the most talked-about painting in the Pre-Raphaelite era. Describing the scene as 'the vilest cabaret in France', the writer Charles Dickens led the charge, offended by the use of a contemporary setting for a religious scene. It was perceived as being linked to the Oxford Movement, a group within the Church of England that sought a restoration of elements of Catholicism, most notably the Sacraments, anathema to many people at the time.

WH Hunt, *Rienzi Vowing to Obtain Justice for the Death of his Young Brother, Slain in a Skirmish Between the Colonna and Orsini Factions*, oil on canvas, 1848–9, private collection, 87 x 122cm (34¾ x 44¾in)

This was the first painting in which the initials PRB were appended to Hunt's signature. The picture received a mixed reaction, but the writer Bulwer Lytton, whose novel had inspired the work, praised it. John Gibbons purchased the painting, but before it was delivered Hunt added the figures of the mother and child coming over the hill, top left.

DG Rossetti, *To Caper Nimbly in a Lady's Chamber, to the Lascivious Pleasing of a Lute,* pen and ink, 1850, private collection, 21 x 15cm (8½ x 6in)

Sometime in 1850, Rossetti turned his output towards watercolours and drawing. The small drawing shown here appears to be a preliminary sketch for a later watercolour of *The Borgia Family,* executed in 1863, although the literary source is from the very first scene of Shakespeare's 'Richard III'. George Boyce, Rossetti's artist friend, acquired the drawing.

WH Deverell, *Twelfth Night*, oil on canvas, 1849–50, The Forbes Collection, 102 x 133cm (36¾ x 49in)

This was the first of only a few paintings by Deverell, who was to die tragically young four years after completing it. The scene is from Shakespeare's play of the same name, with the three protagonists modelled by himself as Orsino, Rossetti as Cesario and Lizzie Siddal, who Deverell had discovered working in a milliner's shop, as Viola. The work was acquired by William Bell Scott.

JE Millais, *Ferdinand Lured by Ariel*, oil on panel, 1850, The Makins Collection, 65 x 51cm (26 x 20½ in)

The literary basis for this picture was Shakespeare's *The Tempest*, lines from which were added to the catalogue entry when it was exhibited at the Academy in 1850. The background was Millais' first *en plein air* picture that adhered to the tenets of Pre-Raphaelitism, that is, to 'go to nature'. The incredible detailing extends to the costumes of both Ferdinand and the sprite Ariel, whose elaborate dress is adorned with bats.

WH Hunt, *The Lady of Shalott*, pen, ink and black chalk, 1850, National Gallery of Victoria, Melbourne, Australia, 24 x 14cm (9½ x 5½in)

The Lady of Shalott was a poem written by Alfred Lord Tennyson, first published in 1833. Its theme is Arthurian legend, a favourite motif of the Pre-Raphaelites who were closely acquainted with Tennyson. There are a number of pictures on this subject, but Hunt's focus is reserved for the part in the poem where the Lady of Shalott has been cursed for looking toward Camelot after seeing Sir Lancelot in the magic mirror.

JE Millais, *Lorenzo and Isabella*, oil on canvas, 1848–9, The Walker Art Gallery, Liverpool, UK, 103 x 143cm (37¼ x 53¼in)

The first of Millais' pictures after becoming a Brother, this resembles the paintings of the Italian *quattrocento*. Lines from Keats' poem *Isabella* accompanied the picture in the catalogue entry. There are a number of Symbolist motifs used in the painting such as the blood orange being shared by Isabella and Lorenzo and the passion-flowers around the arch.

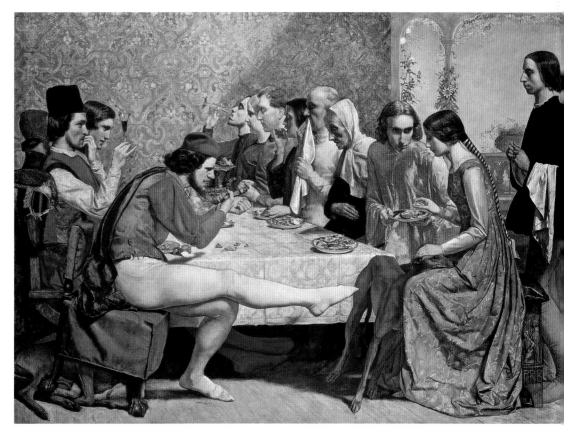

James Collinson, *The Renunciation of the Queen of Hungary*, oil on canvas, 1850, Johannesburg Art Gallery, South Africa, 122 x 184cm (44¾ x 69½in)

A deeply religious and pious man, Collinson began this work as an act of homage to a favourite saint. Elizabeth, later to be Queen of Hungary was married at age 14 in 1221, but widowed at 20, her husband dying while on crusade. Upon hearing the news, she gave up her title and wealth in favour of working with the poor, becoming famous for her Christian charity. She died at the young age of 24, and was later made a saint.

WH Hunt, *Claudio and Isabella*, oil on panel, 1850, Tate Gallery, London, UK, 76 x 43cm (30½ x 17¼in)

Executed between 1850 and 1853, when it was exhibited at the Academy, this painting is based on Shakespeare's *Measure for Measure*.

The artist's friend Augustus Egg, himself a painter of Shakespearean characters, commissioned it. It was later reproduced as an engraving with the moral message of 'Thou shall do no evil that good may come'. The model for Claudio was Walter Deverell.

JE Millais, *The Bridesmaid*, oil on panel, 1851, The Fitzwilliam Museum, Cambridge, UK, 28 x 20cm (11 x 8in)

Unusually for an early Pre-Raphaelite picture, Millais used the services of a professional model for this painting, a Miss McDowall. In other respects it is a painting that begins to define the Pre-Raphaelite aesthetic, through the bright red hair of the sitter and an element of symbolism, in this case the orange blossom around her neck that denotes chastity.

Ford Madox Brown, *Self-portrait*, black chalk, 1850, Walker Art Gallery, Liverpool, UK, 25 x 23cm (10 x 9in)

The quality of Madox Brown's draughtsmanship is clearly demonstrated in this drawing. He had studied the drawings of the masters of this discipline, including Rembrandt and Albrecht Dürer while he was in the Low Countries, and also Leonardo, Raphael and Claude Lorrain, whose work he would have seen in the Louvre during the years 1840–3.

WH Hunt, *A Converted British Family Sheltering a Christian Missionary from the Persecution of the Druids,* oil on canvas, 1849–50, The Ashmolean Museum, Oxford, UK, 111 x 141cm (40¼ x 52½in)

Hunt painted the background to this picture while in Homerton, north-east London, where there are large areas of marshland. The figures, including Rossetti as the missionary, were added later. However, probably due to the discrepancies of his earlier *Eve of St Agnes* picture, Hunt insisted on painting the figures only when the sun was shining.

Charles Collins, *Convent Thoughts,* oil on canvas, 1850–1, The Ashmolean Museum, Oxford, UK, 84 x 59cm (33½ x 23½in)

The attention to detail is incredible in this work. Not only does Collins pursue the Ruskinian ideals of being faithful to nature, but it is possible to read the open pages of the book, depicting images of the Virgin Mary and the crucifixion, that the nun is carrying. Parallels can be drawn between the Virgin and the nun, who is carrying a passionflower, a symbol of Christ's fate.

Ford Madox Brown, *Geoffrey Chaucer Reading the 'Legend of Custance' to Edward III and his Court, at the Palace of Sheen, on the Anniversary of the Black Prince's Forty-fifth Birthday,* oil on canvas, 1847–51, Art Gallery of New South Wales, Sydney, Australia, 372 x 296cm (136½ x 118½in)

Madox Brown's *Chaucer* is the largest painting undertaken by the artist. One critic remarked that it had no 'Pre-Raphaelite nonsense' about it, on seeing it at the Academy in 1851, indicating that it was begun prior to the influence of the Brotherhood. This is also evident in the fact that it has a bitumen base, something that the Pre-Rapahelites railed against.

JE Millais, *Mariana,* oil on mahogany, 1851, Tate Gallery, London, UK, 60 x 50cm (24 x 20in)

Although the character for this painting is taken from Shakespeare's *Measure for Measure,* the lines appended to Millais' picture for the Academy exhibition of 1851 were from Tennyson's poem *Mariana.* In the poem, the central character is frustrated as she waits for her lover, a state contrasting with the stained glass panels that depict the Annunciation. The windows themselves are copies of those at Merton College, Oxford.

Arthur Hughes, *Ophelia,*
oil on canvas, 1852,
Manchester City Art
Gallery, UK, 69 x 124cm
(27½ x 49½ in)

Hughes was only 19 years
old when he painted his
version of Ophelia, which is
very different from the scene
painted by Millais, who
exhibited his picture of the
same name at the Academy
in 1852. Like Millais, however,
great attention to natural
detail was given in this
picture, including green algae
floating on the water's
surface and a bat that
invades the picture to give
it a gothic feel.

WH Hunt, *The Hireling
Shepherd,* oil on canvas,
1851–2, Manchester
City Art Gallery, UK,
76 x 110cm (30½ x 44in)

The title for this painting
comes from St John's
Gospel, and the story of the
good shepherd and the
hireling who would not look

after the sheep. Hunt saw
the metaphor as linked to
the current inability of the
church to look after its 'flock'
properly. The painting depicts

the flirtatious shepherdess
who has been distracted
while the sheep have
wandered into the cornfield
and become bloated.

JE Millais, *The Woodman's Daughter*, oil on canvas, 1851, Guildhall Art Gallery, London, UK, 89 x 65cm (35½ x 26in)

Coventry Patmore's poem *The Woodman's Daughter* was the inspiration for this painting. Millais knew Patmore and they had a mutual appreciation for each other's work. The background was painted in woods near Oxford, while Millais was staying with Thomas Combe, his patron. The models for the picture are not known, and it remained unsold at the end of the Academy exhibition in 1851.

William Dyce, *King Lear and the Fool in the Storm,* oil on canvas, 1851, National Gallery of Scotland, UK, 136 x 173cm (54½ x 69¼ in)

The theme for the picture is taken from Shakespeare's *King Lear.* In the painting a court jester begs Lear to shelter from the storm. Lear, who is elderly and on the verge of insanity, does not listen and invites the storm to sterilize the human race. However, Lear is also paranoid and believes the storm to be at the behest of his daughters, whom he has disinherited.

JE Millais, *A Huguenot on St Bartholomew's Day, Refusing to Shield Himself from Danger by Wearing the Roman Catholic Badge*, oil on canvas, 1851–2, The Makins Collection, 93 x 62cm (37¼ x 25in)

Millais has chosen to depict a fictitious scene of two lovers, set against the background of the massacre of thousands of Protestant Huguenots on St Bartholomew's Day in 1572. The artist has depicted the Huguenot refusing to relinquish his faith, which had strong resonances with Protestant anger at papal aggression in 1850, when the Catholic hierarchy in England was reinstated.

WH Hunt, *Our English Coasts (Strayed Sheep)*, oil on canvas, 1852, Tate Gallery, London, UK, 43 x 58cm (17¼ x 23¼in)

This painting has two titles: the original was for the home market when it was exhibited at the Academy of 1853; later it was changed for the *Exposition Universelle* in 1855 when it was shown as *Strayed Sheep*, possibly to emphasize the religious significance of the picture. The location is a well-known beauty spot, called 'Lovers Seat', on England's south coast at Hastings.

JE Millais, *Ophelia*, oil on canvas, 1851–2, Tate Gallery, London, UK, 76 x 112cm (30½ x 44½in).

Arguably Millais' best-known work, *Ophelia* was created in two separate phases. The flora and fauna background was painted at Worcester Park in the summer and autumn of 1851. The figure of Ophelia was modelled by Lizzie Siddal, who laid in a bath of water that was heated underneath by lamps, in the artist's studio. Lizzie was taken ill with a severe cold during the sitting when the lamps went out.

DG Rossetti, *Rossetti Being Sketched by Elizabeth Siddal,* pen and ink, 1853, private collection, dimensions unknown

Elizabeth Siddal was, at various times, Rossetti's student, as well as his lover. Although she only ever completed one painting, there are several sketches by her in studio settings, and many by Rossetti as studies of her. Unusually, Rossetti portrays himself as the sitter to a sketch by Lizzie. John Ruskin purchased most of Lizzie's sketches.

JE Millais, *The Order of Release*, oil on canvas, 1852–3, Tate Gallery, London, UK, 103 x 74cm (41¼ x 29½in)

Millais continued the theme of love in difficult circumstances, following on from the success of *A Huguenot* the previous year. In this picture a bare-footed wife, modelled by Effie Ruskin, herself a Scot, secures the release of her husband, a Jacobite rebel who has been an English prisoner of war. It is perhaps prophetic that Effie was to seek a release from her own marriage the following year.

WH Hunt, *The Light of the World,* oil on canvas, 1851–3, Keble College, Oxford, UK, 125 x 60cm (50 x 24in)

This is the initial version of Hunt's first religious, and arguably his most famous, picture. Because of Hunt's attention to detail, the work took two years to execute. The outside detail was painted from nature, at the site of an old, abandoned hut in Worcester Park, Surrey. Hunt recalled in his diary that it was painted in November, when it was bitterly cold.

JE Millais, *The Proscribed Royalist, 1651*, oil on canvas, 1852–3, private collection, 103 x 74cm (41¼ x 29½in)

This painting was exhibited at the Academy in 1853, where it hung alongside its pendant (companion piece) *The Order of Release*. It depicts a Royalist who has been condemned to death during the English Civil War. His lover, who is seen passing bread to him, is a Puritan and thus on the opposing side. It has been suggested that Millais may well have been inspired by a contemporary opera of the time, Bellini's *I Puritani*.

DG Rossetti, *Arthur's Tomb,* pencil, pen and ink and watercolour on paper, 1854, private collection, 24 x 38cm (9½in x 15in)

The scene for this watercolour is based on, but not faithful to, Malory's *Le Morte d'Arthur*, a key text for Pre-Raphaelite inspiration. In the book, Lancelot and Guinevere are surrounded by courtiers, suggesting that the picture is intended as a reflective work on the perils of adulterous affairs. Perhaps Rossetti was warning of the repercussions that Millais' impending and scandalous affair with Effie Ruskin would have.

JE Millais, *The Waterfall at Glenfinlas,* oil on panel, 1853, Delaware Art Museum, USA, 23 x 34cm (9 x 13½in)

In 1853, Millais went on his now infamous tour of the Scottish Highlands with the Ruskins, essentially to paint the writer's portrait. He began this small panel as a preparatory work in order to perfect the rocks and running water that would form the background for the much larger portrait. Both pictures are exemplary in their depiction of the natural surrounding, a testament to Ruskin's tenets.

Arthur Hughes, *Fair Rosamund,* oil on panel, 1854, National Gallery of Victoria, Melbourne, Australia, 40 x 31cm (16 x 12½in)

The sixteenth century *Ballad of Fair Rosamund* is the basis for the legend of King Henry II's mistress, in which it is suggested that the King's jealous wife, Eleanor of Aquitaine, poisoned her. Hughes has alluded to this in his painting depicting Rosamund in the foreground, being watched by the Queen at the doorway. Poisonous flowers can be seen in the verges alongside the path back to the castle.

JE Millais, *Waiting,* oil on panel, 1854, Birmingham Museum and Art Gallery, UK, 32 x 25cm (12½ x 12¾in)

Since *Waiting* was not shown in public during Millais' lifetime, it can be assumed that this cabinet-sized picture was personal. At the time of the painting, Millais was keeping a low profile, awaiting the outcome of Effie Ruskin's annulment proceedings against her husband, and keeping a safe distance from her in the interim. They were re-united in the winter of 1854–5 and married later that year.

DG Rossetti, *The First Anniversary of the Death of Beatrice,* watercolour, 1853–4, The Ashmolean Museum, Oxford, UK, 42 x 61cm (40¾ x 24½in)

The largest of Rossetti's watercolours at the time it was painted, this painting depicts the moment when Dante's friends have come to commiserate with him on the first anniversary of the death of Beatrice. The artist's brother, William, modelled for Dante and Lizzie Siddal posed for the female visitor, who is possibly meant to be Gemma Donati, Dante's subsequent bride.

DG Rossetti, *Portrait of Elizabeth Siddal,* watercolour, 1854, Delaware Art Museum, USA, 18 x 16cm (7 x 6¼in)

In 1854, Ruskin was urging Rossetti to marry Lizzie, which the latter may well have considered except for her continued ill health. She went away to convalesce in 1856, and on her return they became engaged. It was not until 1860 that they married, the intervening years marred by Lizzie's continued illnesses and depression that were eventually to take their toll only two years later.

WH Hunt, *Cairo: Sunset on the Gebel Mokattum,* watercolour, 1854, The Whitworth Art Gallery, Manchester, UK, 17 x 37cm (6½ x 14¾in)

Hunt exhibited this small watercolour at a private Pre-Raphaelite exhibition on his return from the Holy Land in 1857. He chose not to exhibit at the Academy, possibly because they had rejected his application for membership the previous year. The picture is one of a series of landscapes painted on his arrival in Egypt in 1854. His enchantment with this new and alien landscape is evident in these watercolours, with their vibrant use of colour and light.

Ford Madox Brown, *An English Autumn Afternoon*, oil on canvas, 1852–4, Birmingham Museum and Art Gallery, UK, 72 x 135cm (28½ x 54in)

During June 1852, Madox Brown moved his studio to the suburbs of London, Hampstead, with far-reaching views toward the city. The location had already provided inspiration for the painter John Constable earlier in the century.

Brown's painting is far more meticulous in detailing the flora and fauna, but lacks the atmosphere of Constable's versions, particularly in the rendition of light on the landscape.

WH Hunt, *The Sphinx, Gizeh, Looking Towards the Pyramids at Sakhara*, 1854, Harris Museum, Preston, UK, 25 x 36cm (10 x 14½in)

Hunt's enthusiasm for 'looking to nature' is evident in this watercolour, which is unusual for focusing on the rear view of the Sphinx. The image clearly displays the geological strata of the region, a facet of the area that is not the usual focus of tourists. In his memoirs, Hunt stated that he gave consideration to the fact that the Sphinx was facing east towards the Holy Land, his next destination.

INTO THE
MAINSTREAM 1855–60

Despite their early detractors, some of the Pre-Raphaelite artists were by now part of the mainstream. Millais had moved away from the group and was pursuing a career as a member of the Academy he had once rebelled against. Rossetti, in contrast, continued to reject the Academy in favour of private patronage, as his own aesthetic moved towards a more contemplative mode of depiction. He also began a second wave of Pre-Raphaelitism that encouraged a younger generation, such as Morris and Burne-Jones, to use the aesthetic. Fresh from his first visit to the Holy Land, Holman Hunt continued to explore themes of a spiritual nature, mainly related to biblical narratives.

Left: JE Millais, The Rescue, *oil on canvas, 1855, The National Gallery of Victoria, Melbourne, Australia, 122 x 84cm (48¾ x 33⅓in)*
Above: Charles Collins, The Good Harvest of 1854, *oil on canvas, 1854, The Victoria and Albert Museum, London, dimensions unknown*

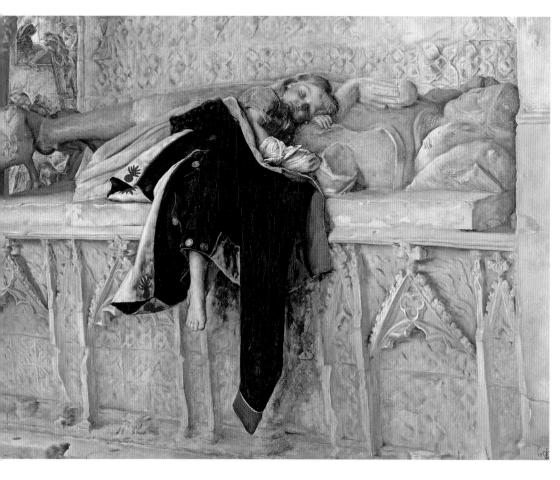

JE Millais, *L'Enfant du Regiment*, oil on paper, 1855, Yale Centre for British Art, USA, 46 x 62cm (18½ x 25in)

In the autumn of 1854, Millais was staying at Winchelsea where he began this painting, although the young girl was added the following year when he was in Scotland. The tomb she is laying on is from the local parish church and dates from the late thirteenth century. Millais was inspired to paint this picture after seeing Donizetti's opera *La Fille du Regiment*, first performed in England in 1847.

DG Rossetti, *Portrait of Robert Browning*, pencil and watercolour, 1855, Fitzwilliam Museum, Cambridge, UK, 12 x 11cm (4½ x 4¼in)

Rossetti was already an admirer of Browning's poetry, when he met him in 1851. Thereafter they were often in each other's company, finding familiar ground through their shared interests in medievalism and medieval Italian culture. They travelled to Paris, France, where Browning's knowledge of early Italian Renaissance art was, according to Rossetti, 'beyond that of anyone else I ever met'.

Ford Madox Brown, *The Last of England,* oil on panel, 1852–5, Birmingham Museum and Art Gallery, UK, 83 x 75cm (33 x 30in)

When Thomas Woolner, one of the original members of the PRB, decided to emigrate to Australia, Madox Brown was inspired to paint this image, a non-sentimental scene of a married couple's departure from England that is nevertheless full of pathos. His wordy catalogue entry for the Liverpool Academy Exhibition of 1856 states that: 'the husband broods bitterly over blighted hopes and severance from all he has been striving for'. Woolner was one of many thousands who migrated to Australia and the United States at this time.

John William Inchbold, *The White Doe of Rylstone,* oil on canvas, 1852–5, Leeds Museum and Art Gallery, UK, 69 x 51cm (27½ x 20½in)

Many of Inchbold's paintings feature landscape scenes of England and also Switzerland, where he travelled with Ruskin in 1856 and 1858. The inspiration for this painting is from William Wordsworth's narrative poem of the same name, published in 1815. The painting is also entitled *From Bolton,* two words from the first line of the poem, referring to the ruins of Bolton Priory, which may well form the backdrop to this picture.

William Shakespeare Burton, *The Wounded Cavalier*, oil on canvas, 1855, Guildhall Art Gallery, London, UK, 89 x 104cm (35½in x 41½in)

Apart from this picture, Burton is not known as a Pre-Raphaelite painter, most of his other works being genre and history painting in a traditional Academy style. The painting, set during the English Civil War, depicts a Puritan woman tending to a wounded cavalier soldier while her husband, carrying an over-large Bible, looks on jealously. The picture was well received at the Academy of 1856, where it was hung next to Hunt's *The Scapegoat*.

WH Hunt, *The Scapegoat*, oil on canvas, 1854–5, Manchester Art Gallery, UK, 34 x 46cm (13½in x 18½in)

There are two versions of this picture, this being the smaller version which was begun slightly earlier, possibly as a test. The inspiration for this painting came from the Bible, which Hunt was avidly reading at the time, more specifically the Book of Leviticus, which talks of a scapegoat being sent into the wilderness, bearing all the sins of the people of Israel. The painting was executed mainly along the shores of the Dead Sea during Hunt's time in Israel.

DG Rossetti, *Self-portrait*, pen and ink, 1855, Fitzwilliam Museum, Cambridge, UK, 13 x 12cm (5 x 4½in)

The strong draughtsmanship of this drawing is a testament to the influence of Ruskin as Rossetti's mentor at the time it was executed. The portrait shows an artist beginning his mature years full of confidence, but still retaining something of his arrogant Bohemianism. Ruskin himself was also a consummate draughtsman, and would not have allowed Rossetti to become indolent under his mentorship, which lasted until 1864.

Ford Madox Brown, *Waiting: An English Fireside,* oil on panel, 1851–5, Walker Art Gallery, Liverpool, UK 31 x 20cm (12½ x 8in)

This painting is of Madox Brown's second wife, Emma Hill, and his daughter Catherine born in 1850. Originally it was intended as a cabinet picture, but sometime in 1854 or 1855, the artist added to the painting, to depict a woman waiting for her soldier husband to return from the Crimean War. His portrait miniature lies on the table, and the gloomy shadow on the wall creates a feeling of tension and anxiety.

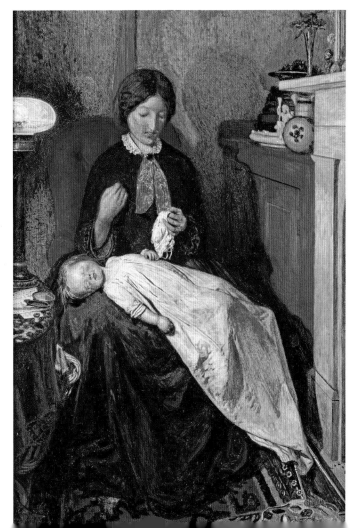

WH Hunt, *Plain of Rephaim from Zion,* watercolour, 1855, Whitworth Art Gallery, Manchester, UK, 36 x 51cm (14½ x 20½in)

This is one of a series of five watercolours that Hunt executed at the beginning of his tour to the Holy Land; he also designed beautiful gilt frames for the paintings that he felt encapsulated aspects of the area. Rephaim is a plain in Judah, and is supposedly the site where David fought his battles with the Philistines, including his famous encounter with their champion, Goliath. Hunt would have been well aware of the significance of this site.

Ford Madox Brown, *Heath Street, Hampstead,* oil on canvas, 1852–5, Manchester Art Gallery, UK, 23 x 31cm (9 x 12½in)

A small oil painting that provided a template for Madox Brown's major painting *Work,* this was painted *en plein air* in the summer of 1852. The painting was reworked in 1855 when the figure of the butcher's boy was added. In the intervening years, Madox Brown moved from Hampstead to a new studio in nearby Kentish Town. Much of the location depicted in this scene can still be recognized today.

Ford Madox Brown, *Windermere*, oil on canvas, 1855, Lady Lever Art Gallery, Liverpool, UK, 18 x 49cm (7 x 19½in)

One of Madox Brown's traits as an artist was to create unusual shapes for his pictures, most notably in *The Last of England* and *An English Autumn Afternoon*. In this painting, the canvas has been altered, cutting down the sky to create a long narrow panoramic format. Originally, an oval mount, the outline of which can still be seen in the slightly faded image, masked the larger painting.

William Bell Scott, *The Trial of William Wallace,* oil on canvas, date unknown, Guildhall Art Gallery, London, UK, 137 x 185cm (54½ x 70in)

This romanticized tableau of the trial depicts a defiant William Wallace, the rebel Scot who dared to defy King Edward I in several battles for Scottish independence in the late 13th century. He was eventually brought to London for trial before being brutally executed. Two books about Wallace were written in the early 19th century that the artist might have read, one of them by Sir Walter Scott.

Arthur Hughes, *April Love*,
oil on canvas, 1855–6, Tate
Gallery, London, UK,
89 x 50cm (35½ x 20in)

William Morris, who was still
a student at Oxford,
purchased this painting from
the Academy Exhibition of
1856. It was much admired
by Ruskin who called it
'exquisite in every way'.
The scene is based on
Tennyson's *The Miller's
Daughter*, and depicts the
essence of young love.
The girl is modelled by
Tryphena Foord, who
married Hughes the year
this was painted.

Ford Madox Brown, *William
Michael Rossetti, Painted by
Lamplight*, oil on panel,
1856, Wightwick Manor,
Wolverhampton, UK,
17 x 17cm (6½ x 6½in)

Much of what we know
about the Pre-Raphaelites is
due to William Rossetti,
who published the letters
and diaries of his older
brother Dante, and Madox
Brown, together with the
PRB journal which he ran
between 1849 and 1853; all
of which provide insight into
the lives of the Brothers.
William was later married to
Madox Brown's daughter
Lucy in 1874, when he was
45 and she was 31.

WH Hunt, *Fairlight Downs, Sunlight on the Sea,* oil on panel, 1852–8, private collection, 23 x 31cm (9 x 12½in)

The long gestation period of this painting suggests that Hunt had difficulty with some aspects of the picture, as mentioned several times in the artist's correspondence. At one point it was even offered to his dentist in settlement of a treatment bill, but Hunt seems to have considered the work too valuable, despite its diminuitive size. It was first exhibited in 1858 at Ernest Gambart's exhibition of 'cabinet pictures, sketches and watercolour drawings' in London.

JE Millais, *Autumn Leaves,* oil on canvas, 1856, Manchester Art Gallery, UK, 104 x 74cm (41½ x 29½in)

Millais wrote to Frederic Stephens that he wished for *Autumn Leaves* to be a 'picture to awaken by its solemnity the deepest religious reflection'. The resulting picture is of contemplation, one that considers mood over and above any narrative intent. It is very much a precursor to Millais' developing brand of Aestheticism. The idea for the picture came from watching Tennyson burning leaves in his own garden the previous year.

JE Millais, *The Blind Girl,* oil on canvas, 1854–6, Birmingham Museum and Art Gallery, 83 x 62cm (33 x 25in)

This is the first of Millais paintings to be described as 'pathetic' due to its sentimentality. Without the use of her eyes, the blind girl is having to employ her other senses in order to enjoy the scene around her; the smell of the damp air and grass after the storm, the sound of the crows and sheep in the background and the touch of a flower through her fingertips. Her companion is probably explaining the colours of the rainbow set against the dark sky.

JE Millais, *Peace Concluded 1856*, oil on canvas, 1856, 117 x 91cm (46½ x 36½in)

Millais reprised his familiar motif of the vulnerable male and stoical female in this picture about a father's return from the Crimean War, which had ended that year. The two daughters, one of whom engages with the viewer, are valorizing their wounded father. The girl on the right holds her father's campaign medal, while her sister proffers the dove of peace. The dog at the man's feet symbolizes the fidelity of the married couple.

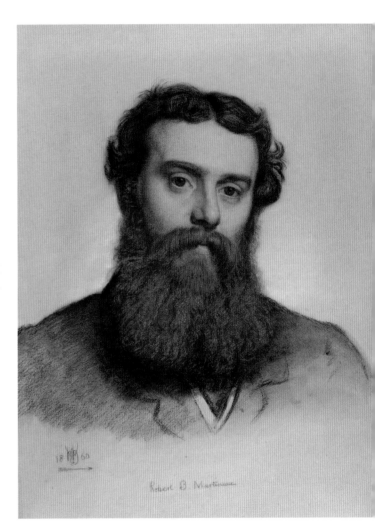

WH Hunt, *Robert Braithwaite Martineau*, pencil, c.1860, Walker Art Gallery, Liverpool, UK, dimensions unknown

Sometime in 1851, Millais had persuaded Hunt to take Martineau on as a pupil. The resulting friendship lasted until Martineau's death in 1869. Martineaus's most famous work, *The Last Day in the Old Home*, was a standard Academy genre picture not in a Pre-Raphaelite style. The painting showed a young aristocrat who had gambled away the family fortune, a moralistic narrative that clearly showed Hunt's influence.

Ford Madox Brown, *Cromwell on his Farm at St Ives, 1636*, pastel, gouache, ink and pencil, 1853–6, Whitworth Art Gallery, Manchester, UK, 35 x 25cm (14 x 10in)

This modestly sized drawing started life as an idea for a large-scale history painting that was not undertaken for another twenty years. It depicts Oliver Cromwell on his farm in Huntingdon about four years before his move to London and the beginning of the English civil war, in which he became the leader of the Parliamentary forces against King Charles II.

Henry Wallis, *The Death of Chatterton*, oil on canvas, 1856, Yale Centre for British Art, USA, 23 x 30cm (9 x 12in)

Wallis did not produce many paintings in the Pre-Raphaelite mode, but this is his most famous. The scene depicts the death of Thomas Chatterton, a minor poet and writer of the eighteenth century who took his own life at 17 years of age, after failing to make a success of himself in London. He lived and died in a garret, as shown in this work with its view of St Paul's Cathedral and the City of London in the background.

JE Millais, *Alice Gray*, oil on canvas, 1857, private collection, 31 x 20cm (12½ x 8in)

Alice Gray, Millais' youngest sister-in-law, sat for this delightful portrait when she was eleven years of age. She modelled for several pictures by Millais, including *Autumn Leaves* and *Apple Blossoms – Spring*. It was at this time that Millais realized the beauty of the subject matter; writing to Charles Collins 'The *only* head you could paint to be considered beautiful by *everybody* would be the face of a small girl about eight years old'.

DG Rossetti, *The Blue Closet,* watercolour, 1857, Tate Gallery, London, UK, 35 x 26cm (14 x 10½in)

At the time this was painted, Rossetti was working on his drawings for the Moxon Tennyson, which may well have provided the inspiration for this work, if not the actual narrative. His contribution to the book was an illustration to accompany Tennyson's *The Palace of Art*, entitled *King Arthur and the Weeping Queens*. In this watercolour, Rossetti has replaced Arthur with a strange musical instrument which serves to convey the essence of a mournful ballad.

JE Millais, *A Dream of the Past – Sir Isumbras at the Ford*, oil on canvas, 1857, Lady Lever Art Gallery, Liverpool, UK, 126 x 172cm (50½ x 68½in)

Ruskin thoroughly disliked this painting, seeing it as proof that Millais was moving away from truth to nature in favour of a new aesthetic, one that embraced the purely spiritual. It was what Ruskin referred to earlier in his *Modern Painters* as the 'pathetic fallacy', in which inanimate objects are afforded human characteristics. Millais has, for theatrical effect, subverted the natural play of light by highlighting the armour and the children's faces, despite the fact there is no corresponding light source.

WH Hunt, *Edward Lear,*
pencil, 1857, Walker Art
Gallery, Liverpool, UK,
63 x 50cm (25½ x 20in)

Edward Lear was introduced
to Hunt in 1852 by
Martineau and, like him,
became one of his pupils.
His lessons were in exchange
for teaching Hunt Italian.
Lear was a writer and later
became an illustrator, having
developed his early talent for
drawing. He is particularly
well known for his nonsense
poems, including *The Owl
and the Pussycat.*

JE Millais, *The Escape of a
Heretic, 1559*, oil on canvas,
1857, Museo de Arte de
Ponce, Puerto Rico,
106 x 76cm (42½ x 30½in)

During their time in Scotland
between 1855 and 1857, the
newly wedded Millais and
Effie visited the historian Sir
William Stirling, a specialist in
Spanish history. Millais may
well have gained an insight
into the Inquisition from
their conversations which
inspired this picture, showing
a young woman, wearing a
convicted heretic's penitential
garment, being freed by a
man who has gagged the
priest hearing her confession.

DG Rossetti, *Sir Lancelot's Vision*, watercolour, 1857, Ashmolean Museum, Oxford, UK, 71 x 107cm (28½ x43in)

The Oxford Union murals produced in 1857 have now largely faded, and are not available for viewing by the general public. There are some preparatory drawings and watercolours, however, including this one that demonstrates Rossetti's fresco style. The large patches of white are where the clerestory windows are situated in the hall.

Ford Madox Brown, *Stages of Cruelty,* oil on canvas, 1856–7, Manchester City Art Gallery, UK, 73 x 60cm (29¼ x 24in)

This painting was begun in the summer of 1856, when only the wall and the lilacs behind it were completed. It was not finished until the following year, with the main figure being modelled on Madox Brown's daughter, Lucy. The painting was left unfinished until 1890, when it was completed for a commission. Thomas Woolner modeled for the young man's head, and much of the detail of the child was taken from Madox Brown's younger daughter, Catherine.

JE Millais, *News from Home,*
oil on panel, 1856–7,
Walters Art Museum, USA,
36 x 25cm (14½ x 10in)

This painting depicts a
Scottish soldier fighting in
the Crimean War, reading a
letter containing news from
his loved ones at home.

The soldier is of the 42nd
Royal Highland Regiment,
better known as The Black
Watch, who had distinguished
themselves well in Crimea at
the Battle of the Alma in
1854. The painting was
ridiculed by Ruskin, who was
critical of the soldier's
immaculate appearance.

Ford Madox Brown, *Italian
Fisher Boy,* oil on paper,
c.1858, private collection,
18 x 17cm (7 x 6½in)

This painting was
started in 1836 but
subsequently abandoned by
the artist until 1858, when it
was finished and exhibited at
the Liverpool Academy.
WD Holt, a member of a

prominent Liverpool-based
shipping family, purchased it
for the modest price of
fifteen guineas. Madox
Brown had ceased to
show paintings at the
Royal Academy by this time,
partly because of Ruskin's
antagonism toward him,
preferring instead to show
his paintings at smaller
regional and private galleries.

DG Rossetti, *Mary at the
House of St John,*
watercolour, 1858,
Delaware Art Museum,
USA, 46 x 36cm
(18½ x 14½in)

It was always believed that
following the death of Jesus,
Mary, his mother, lived in a
house built for her by

St John, one of the twelve
apostles. Mary is seen here
in her traditional mode of
depiction, spinning wool.
Traditionally, it is John who
witnesses the Assumption of
Mary to heaven, being the
last of the disciples. Rossetti
has added words from
St John's Gospel around
the picture's frame.

William Bell Scott, *Portrait of Algernon Charles Swinburne,* oil on canvas, 1860, Balliol College, Oxford, UK, 47 x 32cm (18¾ x 12¾in)

Swinburne was staying with Bell Scott in Newcastle at the time of this painting. The background is likely to be the Northumbrian coastline, as Scott was working on the series of murals for Wallington Hall, Northumberland, at the time. Swinburne was part of the owner of Wallington Hall, Lady Trevelyan's, inner circle. He was a controversial writer in his day and often described as one of the Decadents alongside Oscar Wilde.

Ford Madox Brown, *Pretty Baa Lambs,* oil on panel, 1851–9, Birmingham Museum and Art Gallery, 61 x 76cm (24½ x 30½in)

When Madox Brown first came into contact with the Pre-Raphaelites he was very enthusiastic about their experiments with painting over a white ground. *Pretty Baa Lambs* was his first painting using this technique, and his first work produced out of doors, direct from nature. Unlike Millais and Hunt, he also painted the figures in the bright sun. It was heavily criticized at the Academy of 1852 when it was first shown, and remained unsold until it was reworked in 1858–9 for his patron James Leathart.

Arthur Hughes, *The Annunciation,* oil on canvas, 1857–8, Birmingham Museum and Art Gallery, 61 x 36cm (24½ x 14½in)

Between 1857 and 1858, Hughes completed a pair of pictures based on religious themes, this one and a Nativity scene, intended as pendants. Structurally and stylistically, they are reminiscent of early Renaissance paintings, but the pointed arch and the costumes are clearly derived from medieval ideas. This picture is full of symbolism, the lilies suggesting the Virgin's purity and a trailing vine which has been used as a Christian motif since the early art of the Byzantines.

DG Rossetti, *Bocca Baciata*, oil on panel, 1859, Museum of Fine Arts, Boston, USA, 32 × 27cm (12½ × 10½in)

Modeled by Fanny Cornforth, this painting was executed as a commission for Rossetti's friend George Boyce. It is named after a phrase used by the Italian poet Giovanni Boccaccio that translates as 'the lips that have been kissed'. The painting marks a transition in Rossetti's *oeuvre*, when he is exploring feminine beauty for its own sake rather than within a narrative framework. The image conveys a feeling of sensuousness, with the rose in the woman's hair suggesting passion and the apple next to her, temptation.

JE Millais, *Apple Blossoms – Spring,* oil on canvas, 1856–9, Lady Lever Art Gallery, Liverpool, UK, 111 × 173cm (44½ × 69¼in)

Nearly four years in execution, this large-scale painting was begun in Scotland in the spring of 1856. It was completed at a similar time to *The Vale of Rest,* and they hung as pendants at the Academy of 1859. Millais continued the theme of the seasons begun with *Autumn Leaves,* completing the sequence with *Winter Fuel* in 1873, and *St Martin's Summer* in 1878. William Graham owned both *The Vale of Rest* and this picture.

Arthur Hughes, *The Long Engagement*, 1859, oil on canvas, Birmingham Museum and Art Gallery, UK, 105 × 52cm (42 × 21 in)

When Hughes entered this painting at the Academy of 1859, it was exhibited with a quotation from Chaucer rather than its present title, which is suggested by the letters AMY cut into the tree and now overgrown with ivy. The protagonists are a curate and his love, possibly barred from marriage by her middle-class parents, who would have higher aspirations for her than as the wife of this lower-ranking clergyman.

E Burne-Jones, *The Legend of St Frideswide (study)*, oil on panel, 1859, Cheltenham Ladies College, UK, dimensions unknown

This is an oil sketch for a stained glass window designed for the Latin Chapel of Christ Church Cathedral in Oxford.

The priory church of St Frideswide, dedicated to and containing some of her relics, once occupied the site of the Cathedral. The priory church was sacked during the Reformation and remodelled to form a new bishopric of Oxford. St Frideswide is the patron saint of Oxford.

DG Rossetti, *Found*, oil on canvas, 1859, Delaware Art Museum, USA, 76 x 89cm (30½ x 35½in)

The uncompleted *Found* was begun in 1853, and despite two separate patrons asking to purchase it when finished, Rossetti was still working on it up to a year before his death in 1882. It is the only modern-life subject the artist ever attempted, and clearly he felt that this type of subject matter was not suited to his temperament. It depicts a fallen woman in disgrace, and was modelled by Fanny Cornforth, a former prostitute herself.

DG Rossetti, *Mary Magdalene at the Door of Simon the Pharisee*, pen and ink, 1853–9, Fitzwilliam Museum, Cambridge, UK, 53 x 46cm (21½in x 18½in)

Some preparatory drawings suggest that this picture was conceived in 1853, but it was not seen by anyone until at least 1858, although it is known that the fawn was drawn from life in 1859. Burne-Jones modelled for the figure of Christ, who is dining with Simon the Pharisee. Mary Magdalene occupies the house opposite, and on seeing Him runs to Simon's door, followed by her own guests who are mocking her.

WH Hunt, *The Schoolgirl's Hymn*, oil on panel, 1859, Ashmolean Museum, Oxford, UK, 35 x 25cm (14 x 10in)

In the summers of 1858 and 1859, Hunt worked on this picture while staying at Fairlight in Sussex, the model being a farm labourer's daughter, Miriam Wilkinson. Although not a major work, Hunt spent further time on it over the following year and then reworked it again in 1861, despite the fact that it had already been shown at Gambart's gallery in 1859. Thomas Combe eventually purchased the picture.

DG Rossetti, *Dantis Amor*, pen and ink, 1860, Birmingham City Museum and Art Gallery, UK 75 x 81cm (30 x 32½in)

This drawing was planned as a triptych for a settle that belonged to William Morris; the panel here shows Love (Amor) holding a sundial that depicts the time of Beatrice's death. The two inset figures are Christ, from whom the sun's rays emanate, and Beatrice surrounded by the dark night, symbolizing the Amor's transition from Purgatory to Paradise.

WH Hunt, *Asparagus Island*, oil on canvas, 1860, private collection, 20 × 26cm (8 × 10½in)

Hunt loved to paint landscapes, and was arguably the only one of the Pre-Raphaelites who stuck to Ruskin's tenets for his whole career. Asparagus Island is just off the coast of the Lizard Peninsula, in Cornwall, the most southerly part of England. This picture depicts the unusual turquoise water, the white sand and the caves of this area. The island is named after the crop of asparagus that was at one time grown there.

DG Rossetti, *King René's Honeymoon*, oil on canvas, 1860, private collection, dimensions unknown

René of Anjou (1409–1480) was a key player in medieval history, controlling several duchies and minor kingdoms in France and what is now part of Italy. He was also the father of Margaret of Anjou, who married King Henry VI of England. René, also known as Good King René, was an amateur artist and patron of the arts, a passion he shared with his second wife Jeanne.

Ford Madox Brown, *The English Boy,* oil on canvas, 1860, Manchester City Art gallery, UK, 40 x 33cm (16 x 13in)

The sitter for this portrait was Madox Brown's five-year old son, Oliver. Madox Brown completed *The Irish Girl* at the same time as this painting, both intended for his patron Thomas Plint, who wanted them as pendants. He paid one hundred guineas for the two paintings. Plint had also commissioned Madox Brown to paint *Work,* which reflected his belief in the Protestant work ethic; it was completed five years later. Plint owned several other Pre-Raphaelite pictures with moral or religious themes.

JE Millais, *The Black Brunswicker*, oil on canvas, 1860, Lady Lever Art Gallery, Liverpool, UK, 104 x 69cm (41½ x 27½in)

Although Millais moved away from the Pre-Raphaelite aesthetic when he produced this painting, he still retained the attention to detail that he had sought in his earlier paintings, such as *Ophelia*.

This painting has more in common with the neoclassicism employed by artists such as Jean Auguste Dominique Ingres however, particularly in the detailing of the garments. The scene depicts a young Prussian officer leaving to join his regiment at the Battle of Waterloo against Napoleon Bonaparte, whose portrait hangs on the wall.

DG Rossetti, *Hanging the Mistletoe*, oil on panel, 1860, The Makins Collection, 33 x 27cm (13 x 10½in)

The tradition of hanging mistletoe can be linked back to the Druids, who used it to decorate their homes in the winter two thousand years ago. Many pagan customs were brought into Christian tradition during the Victorian era, largely as a result of the writings of Charles Dickens. His book *A Christmas Carol*, published in 1843, embedded the ideas of these traditions in popular culture – in particular the idea that gifts should be offered, especially to those who lived in hardship for the rest of the year.

Ford Madox Brown, *The Irish Girl,* oil on canvas, 1860, Yale Centre for British Art, USA, 29 x 27cm (11¼ x 10½in)

The wake of the Potato Famine of 1845 led to strained relations between the English and the Irish.

Many thousands of Irish people had immigrated to England, and their Roman Catholic beliefs were anathema to most Englishmen. Hunt appears to have cosmetically changed the features of the girl to make the image more appealing.

DG Rossetti, *How They Met Themselves,* gouache, 1851–60, Fitzwilliam Museum, Cambridge, UK, 34 x 27cm (13½ x 10½in)

Rossetti completed this rather macabre drawing while on his honeymoon in 1860, nine years after he had begun the picture. He made the point of double-dating the work, highlighting the link between the drawing's gestation period and the length of his engagement to Lizzie. The image depicts the legend of the doppelgänger, which fascinated Rossetti throughout his lifetime.

WH Hunt, *The Lanternmaker's Courtship,* oil on panel, 1854–60, Manchester City Art Gallery, UK, 29 x 19cm (11½ x 7½in)

During Hunt's first visit to Cairo, he witnessed a scene in which a young man was engaged in a conversation with a young woman. Custom prevented him from lifting her veil and so he pressed his hand against her face in order to interpret her features. The subject interested Hunt who had been struggling to find female models to pose for his paintings.

DG Rossetti, *Regina Cordium,* oil on panel, 1860, Johannesburg Art Gallery, South Africa, 26 x 22cm (10½ x 8¾in)

After completing *Bocca Baciata* in 1859, Rossetti continued to produce bust-length portraits of beautiful women without any narrative justification. This painting depicts Lizzie Siddal clutching a pansy, which comes from the French *pensée*, meaning 'thought'. The use of the flower is symbolic of the fact that Lizzie was occupying Rossetti's inner thoughts at this time. The painting was executed just a few months after the couple had married.

William Bell Scott, *Una and the Lion*, oil on canvas, 1860, The National Gallery of Scotland, UK, 92 x 71cm (36¾ x 28¼in)

The inspiration for this painting was Edmund Spenser's epic poem *The Faerie Queen* published in 1590, in which Princess Una seeks to free her parents who have been imprisoned by a dragon. She is aided by a lion who is captivated by her beauty and acts as her protector. Spencer is considered the poet's poet, and his work was widely disseminated by Wordsworth, Keats and Tennyson.

Frederick Sandys, *Mary Magdalene,* oil on panel, 1858–60, Delaware Art Museum, USA, 34 x 28cm (13½ x 11in)

Sandys was a neighbour and close friend of Rossetti, whose influence can be clearly seen in this picture. The artist has portrayed Mary Magdalene in traditional mode, with long hair and carrying a jar of unguent with which she anointed Jesus's feet. Apart from these clues, the lack of narrative context and the modern background would suggest that Sandys, like Rossetti, was exploring the depiction of beautiful young women for their own sake.

John Brett, *The Hedger,* oil on canvas, 1859–60, private collection, 90 x 70cm (36 x 27¾in)

Hedging has been used to separate fields and roads in England and Wales for centuries, and to provide a barrier for keeping livestock contained. The style of hedging or hedgerow varies across different counties. Brett's picture was painted in Kent, the so-called Garden of England; the hedger is hard at work, while his family approach in the background bringing his lunch.

R B Martineau, *A Girl with a Cat,* oil on panel, 1860, Johannesburg Art Gallery, South Africa, 32 x 23cm (12¾ x 9in)

Despite being a pupil of Hunt, Martineau did not fully embrace the Pre-Raphaelite aesthetic, preferring instead to handle genre subjects. Nevertheless, it is not hard to see the influence of the group in this picture with its meticulous attention to detail. Martineau regularly exhibited at the Royal Academy, and also featured as the gentleman on horseback in Madox Brown's painting *Work.*

E Burne-Jones, *Sidonia von Borke,* watercolour, 1860, Tate Gallery, London, UK, 33 x 17cm (13 x 6½in)

Wilhelm Meinhold's romance had been translated into English in 1849 as *Sidonia the Sorceress,* a tale about a witch that was set in the 17th century. The gothic novel came of age in the Victorian era, and many artists were inspired to depict their demonic protagonists. In this tale Sidonia's beauty causes men to fall hopelessly in love with her and become victims of her excessive cruelty.

Ford Madox Brown, *Manfred on the Jungfrau*, oil on canvas, 1840–61, Manchester Art Gallery, UK, 140 x 115cm (56 x 46in)

This painting is inspired by a scene from Byron's epic poem *Manfred*, and depicts the moment the hero, racked with guilt over a past sin, is on the verge of committing suicide by hurling himself from the Jungfrau, a summit in the Bernese Alps. Byron's poem provided inspiration for other artists and creative minds, and is the inspiration for Tchaikovsky's *Manfred Symphony in B minor*. Madox Brown was initially unhappy with the painting and radically reworked it twenty years after its initial incarnation.

William Dyce, *The Woman of Samaria*, oil on panel, c.1860, Birmingham Museum and Art Gallery, UK, 34 x 48cm (13½ x 19¼in)

Dyce is another artist on the margins of Pre-Raphaelitism who was unable to devote much time to painting canvases, but was involved in several fresco commissions including those at the newly built Houses of Parliament. This painting is biblical in theme, and depicts a scene from the New Testament where Jesus converses with a Samaritan woman, asking her for a drink from the vessel she is carrying.

Frederick Sandys, *Autumn*, oil on canvas, 1860, Norwich Castle Museum, UK, 80 x 109cm (32 x 43½in)

This picture was painted at Norwich, with its castle in the background and the Bishop's Bridge in the middle distance. The main figure is heavily borrowed from Millais' *Sir Isumbras at the Ford*. The picture depicts an old soldier recounting his war experiences to his daughter and grandchild.

DG Rossetti, *Fair Rosamund*, oil on canvas, 1861, National Gallery of Wales, UK, 52 x 42cm (21 x 16¾in)

Unlike Hughes' earlier portrayal of Rosamund, there initially appears to be no narrative to this work. Instead, Rossetti seems to have produced a bust-length portrayal of Fanny Cornforth, his muse and mistress at the time this was painted. There is a subtle reference to the legend of Rosamund, however, in the red cord she is holding. The story states that a red cord was used by Henry II to find Rosamund, his mistress, at the end of a maze that he had constructed to prevent her escape.

E Burne-Jones, *Fair Rosamund and Queen Eleanor*, gouache, 1861, private collection, 48 x 37cm (19¼ x 14½in)

Burne-Jones' version of this motif depicts the moment when Queen Eleanor, wife of King Henry II, has followed the red cord used by her husband to locate his mistress at the end of the maze. The scorned queen confronts a startled and frightened Rosamund, who, according to legend, she subsequently murders.

WH Hunt, *Honest Labour has a Comely Face*, oil on panel, 1861, private collection, 30 x 20cm (12 x 8in)

When Hunt's father died in 1855, the artist agreed to tutor his sister Emily. This is a portrait of her executed at the house they shared in Kensington. According to Hunt, the title comes from a line in the play *Patient Grissil* by Thomas Dekker, a contemporary of Shakespeare. This domestic scene is reminiscent of 17th-century Dutch interiors that demonstrate the Puritanical work ethic that had a resonance with the Anglicanism of Hunt's own society.

DG Rossetti, *Angel Offering a Censer*, stained glass, 1861, All Saints Church, Selsley, UK, dimensions unknown

One of the several stained glass panels made for this church on behalf of 'The Firm'. Rossetti has depicted an angel carrying an incense burner, one of the many ancient church rituals to find its was back into English High Anglicanism. Chained censers are swung back and forth by a priest during prayers, symbolizing the drift of the spoken word toward Heaven, carried by the smoke of the incense.

Ford Madox Brown, *The Crucifixion*, stained glass, 1861, All Saints Church, Selsley, UK, dimensions unknown

This is one of a series of stained glass panels made for a new church designed in the gothic revival style by George Frederick Bodley. The church was one of Bodley's earliest commissions and it is unusual in its use of French styling. Bodley knew the Pre-Raphaelites and wanted to involve William Morris's company in helping to create this neo-gothic masterpiece. This was Morris's first commission for ecclesiastical stained glass.

William Bell Scott, *King Egfrid,* mural, 1861, Wallington Hall, Northumberland, UK, dimensions unknown

Lady Trevelyan, a close friend of Ruskin, commissioned William Bell Scott to create eight scenes of Northumbrian history for her home at Wallington Hall. This picture shows the meeting between Saint Cuthbert and King Egfrid of Northumbria, who is trying to persuade the cleric to become the bishop of Lindisfarne. Cuthbert takes up the call, but is subsequently unable to persuade Egfrid against going to war where he is killed in battle.

DG Rossetti, *The Sermon on the Mount,* (study), pen and ink and watercolour, c.1861, Leeds Museum, UK, 77 x 51cm (30¾ x 20½in)

A preliminary drawing for the stained glass window series at All Saints Church in Selsley, it bears little resemblance to the finished item apart from the Christ figure in the centre modelled by George Meredith, who was also the model for Wallis's *Chatterton*. The other figures were all modelled by Rossetti's coterie at the time, with Lizzie Siddal and Fanny Cornforth as the two Marys, and William Morris as St Peter.

E Burne-Jones, *Merlin and Nimue from* Le Morte d'Arthur, watercolour, 1861, Victoria and Albert Museum, London, UK, dimensions unknown

Fanny Cornforth was the model for the enchantress Nimue, who is trying to imprison Merlin in a grave in this painting. Merlin had powers of sorcery and Nimue aspired to improve her skills by learning from his, but she was wary of his amorous advances. Burne-Jones captures the tension of the scene well in this picture, that takes its inspiration from Sir Thomas Malory's *Le Morte d'Arthur*.

John Brett, *The Mountains of St Gingolph*, watercolour and gouache, 1861, Fitzwilliam Museum, Cambridge, UK, 15 x 34cm (6 x 13½in)

In the 1850s, Brett visited Switzerland to examine Turner's work and was inspired to create this painting. Brett was an avid fan of Turner's work, and in his later career spent most of his time in the south west of England fascinated by the coastline, as Turner had been.

THE SECOND WAVE OF PRE-RAPHAELITISM 1861–1870

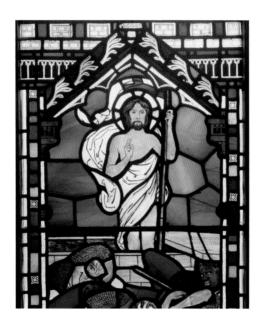

By the early 1860s the second wave of Pre-Raphaelitism was well underway under the direction of Rossetti. By this time, Ruskin was no longer producing his *Academy Notes* in support of his protégés, who included Millais and Rossetti. He was now no longer sympathetic to the newer style that would lead Rossetti and Burne-Jones toward Aestheticism. Holman Hunt and Madox Brown were still stalwart in carrying the torch for the old guard of Pre-Raphaelitism and its 'truth to nature'. Rossetti, Burne-Jones and Madox Brown also developed their artistic talents in other decorative arts.

Left: Arthur Hughes, Home from Work, *oil on canvas, 1861, The Forbes Collection, New York, USA, 103 x 79cm (41¼ x 31½in)*
Above: E Burne-Jones, The Resurrection, *stained glass, 1861, All Saints Church, Selsley, UK, dimensions unknown*

DG Rossetti, *The Annunciation*, oil on panel, 1861–2, St Martin's on the Hill Church, Scarborough, UK, dimensions unknown

Far removed from his 1849 version of this subject, Rossetti's 1861 interpretation of the Annunciation is one based purely on spirituality. The panels decorate the pulpit of St Martin on the Hill Church in the north of England, a testimony to High Anglicanism and the Arts and Crafts aesthetic of William Morris and Co. Rossetti, Brown, Morris, Philip Webb and Burne-Jones created the windows of the church.

DG Rossetti and E Burne-Jones, *The Honeymoon of King René of Anjou,* stained glass, Victoria and Albert Museum, London, UK, 64 x 55cm (25½ x 53¼in)

In the first few years of 'The Firm', Rossetti and Burne-Jones were particularly enthusiastic about stained glass. Morris saw no reason to limit the company's output to ecclesiastical buildings, as this panel demonstrates. Made for the home of the artist Miles Birkett Foster, these are two of a series of four panels designed by Rossetti and Burne-Jones for a cabinet.

Ford Madox Brown, *The Body of Harold Brought Before William the Conqueror,* oil on canvas, 1844–61, Manchester City Art Gallery, UK, 105 x 123cm (42 x 49in)

Madox Brown's submission for the commission to decorate the Houses of Parliament was a cartoon of this painting celebrating one of the most important events in English history. It depicts the body of the defeated King Harold II after being killed by William the Conqueror at the Battle of Hastings in 1066.

WH Hunt, *The Finding of the Saviour in the Temple,* oil on canvas, 1854–61, Walker Art Gallery, Liverpool, UK, 46 x 70cm (18½ x 28¼in)

This is one of Hunt's major pictures and one that had a long gestation period. It was started in 1854 while Hunt was in Jerusalem; the artist insisted that he only use Semitic models for the work. The painting is full of symbolism concerning Jesus's life and resurrection, such as the view across to the Mount of Olives, where he preached his famous sermon.

DG Rossetti, *Joan of Arc Kissing the Sword of Deliverance,* oil on canvas, 1863, Musée des Beaux Arts de Strasbourg, France, 72 x 66cm (28½ x 26½in)

Joan of Arc's piety and emotional strength has long been a source of inspiration for artists. Rossetti's painting depicts Joan, the liberator of France during the Hundred Years War in the fifteenth century, preparing for battle. She is seen kneeling at a small altar, the foot of a crucifix just visible, praying for deliverance. The lily in the picture is not only a symbol of her purity, but also the *fleur de lys,* a symbol of the French kings for whom she is fighting.

Arthur Hughes, *Home From the Sea,* oil on panel, 1856–62, The Ashmolean Museum, Oxford, UK, 51 x 65cm (20½ x 26in)

Although Hughes still adhered to aspects of the Pre-Raphaelite tenet of fidelity to nature at this point in his career, the moral message has gone from this picture, and the viewer is left to consider a simple genre picture. The benefit of this approach is that the image would have had a wider appeal for purchase and also lent itself well to reproduction. This image marks Hughes' transition from painter to illustrator in order to maintain a regular income after he was married in 1855.

JE Millais, *My First Sermon,*
oil on canvas, 1863,
Guildhall Art Gallery,
London, UK,
92 x 77cm (36¾ x 30¾in)

The younger Effie, Millais'
daughter, posed for this
painting, which is often
described as one of his 'fancy
pictures', a term invented by
Sir Joshua Reynolds for
sentimental genre paintings
that usually included children.
Despite the supposedly
saccharine nature of the
piece, Millais was actually
interested in portraying the
loss of childhood, a subject
alluded to in contemporary
novels by Charles Dickens,
from which Millais
took inspiration.

DG Rossetti, *Helen of Troy,*
oil on panel, 1863,
Hamburger Kunstalle,
Germany, 33 x 28cm
(13 x 10¾in)

On the reverse of this
painting, Rossetti has written
in Greek and English 'Helen of
Troy, destroyer of ships,
destroyer of men, destroyer
of cities', a quote from *The
Agamemnon,* the tragedy by
Aeschylus, written in the fifth
century BC. The story, based
on the much earlier *Iliad* and
Odyssey by Homer, tells of the
fall of the ancient city of
Troy because of Helen, the
mythological daughter
of Zeus.

Arthur Hughes, *The Lady with the Lilacs*, oil on panel, 1863, The Art Gallery of Ontario, Canada, 45 x 23cm (18 x 9in)

This painting was owned by Charles Dodgson, a mathematics tutor at Oxford, who became better known as Lewis Carroll, the writer of *Alice in Wonderland*. He was known to several of the Pre-Raphaelites and used his passion for photography to capture most of them for posterity. He had seen some preliminary drawings by Hughes and asked him to execute this painting, which remained one of his favourite pictures.

WH Hunt, *The Afterglow in Egypt*, oil on canvas, 1854–63, Southampton Art Gallery, UK, 185 x 86cm (74 x 34½in)

This painting, dated 1854–63, was begun in Gizeh (Giza) and finished several years later in England. The painting is divided by a line across the centre with the top half painted in Egypt and the bottom half in England, after Hunt added another piece of canvas. The artist had problems with finding any female models for his pictures in the Holy Land, particularly since most of them wore a burka or veil.

DG Rossetti, *My Lady Greensleeves*, oil on panel, 1863, The Fogg Art Museum, USA, 33 x 27cm (13 x10½in)

Rossetti wrote a ballad to accompany this work, a section of which was written on the back of the painting: 'She bound her green sleeve on my helm, Sweet pledge of love's sweet mead'. The inspiration for the image stems from medieval chivalrous protocol, where a knight would wear a lady's detachable sleeve on his helmet to denote his love for her. The model for the picture was Mrs Knewstub, the wife of Rossetti's studio assistant.

DG Rossetti, *The Borgia Family,* watercolour, 1863, Victoria and Albert Museum, London, UK, 52 x 54cm (21 x 21¾in)

One of history's most infamous *femmes fatale* is Lucrezia Borgia (1480–1519) the illegitimate daughter of one of the most powerful families in Valencia, renowned for their corrupt political and sexual machinations at papal level. Rossetti has placed the group in a pose evocative of 16th-century Renaissance portraits. The monkey, again a Renaissance motif, personifies lust, as one of man's baser desires.

E Burne-Jones, *The Merciful Knight,* watercolour and gouache, 1863, Birmingham Museum and Art Gallery, UK, 100 x 69cm (40 x 27½in)

When this work was completed, Burne-Jones's wife Georgiana stated that it appeared to 'sum up and seal the ten years that had passed since Edward went to Oxford'. This picture marked the dawn of a new era in which the artist's style evolved. The scene is inspired by an incident in which an eleventh century Florentine knight, John Gualberto, was miraculously embraced by a wooden figure of Christ while praying.

JE Millais, *Ophelia*, engraving, 1864, private collection, 53 x 86cm (21½ x 34½in)

Henry Graves, the foremost print seller and publisher in London, purchased the copyright to *Ophelia* and selected one of the finest engravers of the period, James Stephenson, to execute a steel engraving of the image. So fine was the resultant work that it was hung at the Academy exhibition of 1866, thus enhancing Millais' popularity in the public's mind.

DG Rossetti, *The Wedding of St George*, watercolour, 1864, Art Gallery of New South Wales, Sydney, Australia, 29 x 35cm (11½ x 14in)

This watercolour is taken directly from a cartoon that Rossetti used to create a stained glass window for Harden Hall in Yorkshire in 1862. It was one of six panels that illustrated the legend of St George and the dragon. The caption on the original glass panel, which read 'How great rejoicing was made for the wedding of St George and the Princess', was omitted from this watercolour.

Simeon Solomon, *Shadrach, Meshac and Abednego*, watercolour, 1863, private collection, 33 x 23cm (13 x 9in)

As a Jewish man, Solomon was interested in the Old Testament stories from the Bible as inspiration for his paintings. This picture tells of 'The Three Young Men' being rescued by a guardian angel from the fiery furnace that King Nebuchadnezzar had cast them into. The three men had displeased the king when they refused to bow down to his golden image in the city.

WH Hunt, *The Children's Holiday: Mrs Fairbairn and her Children,* oil on canvas, 1864, Torre Abbey, Devon, UK, 214 x 147cm (85½ x 58¾in)

Thomas Fairbairn, an avid collector of Victorian art, commissioned Hunt to paint this portrait of his family at their country home in Petworth, Sussex. Due to the sheer size of the commission it is thought that the painting hung at the top of the stairs in the great hall at Burton Park. Fairbairn later inherited his father's baronetcy and was instrumental in establishing the free art gallery in Manchester, which today houses many Pre-Raphaelite works.

DG Rossetti, *The Blue Bower,* oil on canvas, 1865, The Barber Institute, Birmingham, UK, 84 x 71cm (33½ x 28¼in)

Fanny Cornforth posed for this picture dressed in a luxuriant robe undone to reveal white fur beneath, creating a textural quality to the work which is further enhanced by the rich wallpaper behind, an unusual stringed instrument in the foreground and Fanny's riotous hair. The cornflowers on the table may be representative of Rossetti's love for the sitter.

Frederick Sandys, *Morgan Le Fay: Queen of Avalon,* oil on panel, 1863–4, Birmingham Museum and Art Gallery, UK, 62 x 44 cm (25 x 17½in)

In Arthurian legend, Morgan Le Fay was the half sister of Arthur, who practised sorcery against the king because she was jealous of his power. In Sandys' picture she has woven a magic robe which will consume Arthur in fire when he wears it. Her costume is an elaborate mix of styles, including a leopard skin to denote her bestial machinations.

Ford Madox Brown, *King René's Honeymoon,* oil on canvas, 1864, National Gallery of Wales, UK, 62 x 44cm (25 x 17½in)

A cartoon for this work exists as the preliminary drawing for a panel on a painted cabinet that Madox Brown executed for the architect JP Seddon.

Other members of 'The Firm' were also involved in painting the cabinet panels, each of which represented the fine and applied arts. The concept was Madox Brown's, who executed his panel to represent 'architecture'. The painting shown here was completed two years after the cabinet version.

DG Rossetti, *The Beloved*, oil on canvas, 1865–6, Tate Gallery, London, UK, 83 x 76 cm (33 x 30½in)

This painting is based on *The Song of Solomon* from the Old Testament, but is also notable for containing a range of exotic elements. The bride is wearing a Japanese dress and the girl in the foreground is of African origin. The use of large areas of vibrant colour suggests a strong Japanese influence, possibly as the result of the large numbers of *ukiyo-e* (pictures showing everyday life) prints circulating at the time it was painted.

E Burne-Jones, *Cupid and Psyche*, gouache and watercolour, c.1865, Yale Centre for British Art, USA, 70 x 48cm (27 x 19¼in)

This painting is based on the legend of Cupid and Psyche. The goddess Venus is jealous of the beauty of Psyche, a mere mortal, and sends her son Cupid to shoot her with a golden arrow while she is asleep. Venus plans to have an ugly creature at Psyche's side when she wakes, because once she has been struck by Cupid's arrow she will fall in love with the first creature she sees. However, Cupid grazes himself with an arrow and becomes enchanted by Psyche's beauty.

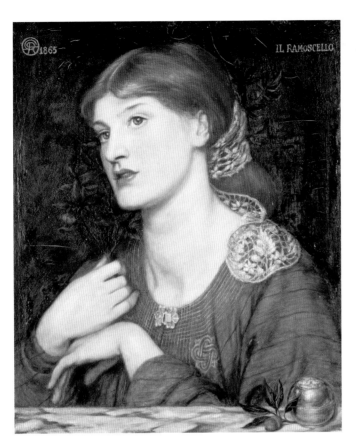

DG Rossetti, *Il Ramoscello,*
oil on canvas, 1865,
Fogg Art Museum, USA,
19 x 16cm (7½ x 6¼in)

It is not certain who was the sitter for this painting, but it has been suggested it was Rossetti's patron William Graham's daughter. Apparently Graham was dissatisfied with the finished work and returned it to the artist for retouching. Graham's other daughter later denied it was of her sister, but that may well be from lack of satisfaction with the portrait in the first place.

E Burne-Jones, *St Cecilia,*
ceramic tile, c.1865,
Fitzwilliam Museum,
Cambridge, UK,
dimensions unknown

Although Burne-Jones designed this tile it was executed by Kate Faulkner, the sister of Charles, one of the founders of 'The Firm'. The tile depicts St Cecilia, the patron saint of church music, holding a manuscript. The legend of her martyrdom suggests that when she was executed, just before she died she was singing praises to God.

E Burne-Jones, *Astrologia,*
gouache, 1865,
private collection,
55 x 47cm (53¼ x 18¾in)

The age-old techniques for
predicting the future by the
study of the solar system and
other matrices were
commonly practised in the
19th century. Burne-Jones
conflates ideas of astrology
with clairvoyance in this
picture, with the central
occultist figure gazing into a
crystal ball. The figure was
modelled by Augusta Jones.

DG Rossetti, *Hesterna Rosa,*
watercolour, 1865,
Delaware Art Museum, USA,
27 x 38cm (10½ x 15in)

A preliminary drawing for
this work, dated 1853, was
given to Rossetti's Brother,
Frederic Stephens. It was
appended with lines from
the 19th-century dramatist
Sir Henry Taylor, added to
the bottom margin: 'Lead we
not here a jolly life, Betwixt
the shine and shade?' This
painting was later developed
from the drawing, showing
Rossetti's tendency to return
to ideas throughout his
career.

Ford Madox Brown, *Work*, oil on canvas, 1852–65, Manchester Art Gallery, UK, 137 x 197cm (54¾ x 73in)

This masterpiece was completed in 1865 for Thomas Plint, a very pious and evangelical collector who supported the Victorian notion of the work ethic as a reflection of Christian virtue. The painting makes several references to contemporary life, the Irish 'navvies' working on the road and the inclusion of such notables as Thomas Carlyle and FD Maurice overseeing from the pavement.

DG Rossetti, *Regina Cordium*, oil on canvas, 1866, Glasgow Art Gallery, UK, 60 x 50cm (24 x 20in)

One of Rossetti's regular models at this time was Alexa Wilding, a girl he had accosted in the street. She was paid a retainer by the artist and sat for many of his best-known pictures. The theme of this painting, 'the Queen of Hearts', had already been explored in earlier paintings. Here, Rossetti includes Cupid in the top right, but the pink roses symbolize admiration rather than love.

DG Rossetti, *Christina Rossetti,* coloured chalks, 1866, Fitzwilliam Museum, Cambridge, UK, 49 x 43cm (19½ x 17¼in)

This rather joyless portrait of the artist's sister reflects the fact that she had recently rejected a suitor, Charles Cayley, with whom she was not in accord on religious grounds. The very devout Christina was never married and stayed at home without enjoying the social group around her brothers. Her devotional poems reflect this, her best-known pieces being *Goblin Market* and the Christmas carol *In the Bleak Mid-winter.*

E Burne-Jones, *Princess Sabra Led to the Dragon,* oil on canvas, private collection, 108 x 97cm (43¼ x 39in)

In this painting, Burne-Jones has portrayed one of the many variants of the tale of St George and the dragon. The dragon occupies a lake used by a local town as its only source of water. In exchange for use of the lake they provide the dragon with one human sacrifice per day. The selection is made by lottery, and on this day the town's Princess, Sabra, has been chosen.

Arthur Hughes, *The Guarded Bower,* oil on canvas, 1866, Bristol City Museum, UK, 118 x 70cm (47 x 27¾in)

The 'bower' referred to in this painting's title is the private space or boudoir of the lady. The private setting is suggestive of an amorous and clandestine relationship, with medieval overtones. The sword wielded by the man guards the lady from the viewer, with whom she seems to be engaging, and also implies ownership. The inclusion of the doves to the bottom right of the picture is ambiguous, as they can be used to suggest lust, as used in pictures of Venus, but can also denote chastity and innocence.

E Burne-Jones, *The Fight: St George Kills the Dragon*, oil on canvas, 1866, Art Gallery of New South Wales, Sydney, Australia, 105 x 131cm (42 x 52½in)

In this portrayal of the legend, the diminuitive dragon appears to be a rather easy foe for the knight, who easily straddles the creature. The tonal values of the painting are ethereal, providing a sense of other-worldliness to the drama, and the picture is regarded as one of Burne-Jones's finest. Miles Birkett Foster commissioned the painting for his home.

DG Rossetti, *Aspecta Medusa*, coloured chalk, private collection, 55 x 51cm (20 x 20½in)

This delicate chalk drawing by Rossetti was one of several he produced based on the subject of the Medusa. It was begun in 1865 and accompanied by a poem of the same name, written by Rossetti. Alexa Wilding sat for the figure of Andromeda and in this drawing, only her head and shoulders are shown. Frederick Leyland, Rossetti's patron, originally owned the drawing.

Frederick Sandys, *Perdita*, oil on panel, c.1866, private collection, dimensions unknown

Inspired by the Shakespearean heroine from *The Winter's Tale*, Sandys' Perdita is portrayed as a beautiful sixteen-year-old girl. In the play, Perdita is a naive and simple girl who is unaware that she is actually a princess. Her suitor, Prince Florizel, is also unaware of her royal blood and his father refuses to consent to their marriage. The couple elope to Sicily and it is not until many years later that Perdita's true identity is discovered.

WH Hunt, *Il Dolce Far Niente*, oil on canvas, 1866, The Forbes Collection, New York, USA, 100 x 82cm (40 x 33in)

The title of this painting, meaning 'sweet and pleasant nothingness', departs from Hunt's usual mode of narrative painting, suggesting that Rossetti had at least some influence on him at the time it was produced, despite their differences. The model was originally Annie Miller, but after meeting and falling in love with Fanny Waugh, Hunt over-painted the face with hers, although the figure retained Annie's hair.

Ford Madox Brown, *St Oswald Receiving St Aidan*, oil on canvas, 1864–6, Lady Lever Gallery, Liverpool, UK, 57 x 52cm (23 x 21in)

Madox Brown was commissioned by 'The Firm' to design a series of stained glass panels for a church in Durham. The motif of this preparatory painting is that of Saint Oswald, a past king of Northumbria, who promulgated the Christian faith to his subjects. The painting shown here was executed at the same time as the glass panel, but was possibly painted by one of the artist's very competent daughters.

DG Rossetti, *The Loving Cup,* gouache, c.1867, Art Gallery of South Australia, Adelaide, Australia, 53 x 36cm (21½ x 14½in)

Rossetti made four copies of this painting in the same year, one in oil for his patron Frederick Leyland, and three others in watercolour, attesting to the images' popularity. Alexa Wilding modelled for the oil version, but Ellen Smith sat for the other three. The artist has returned to a medieval theme, although the sitter appears to be in an Arts and Crafts setting.

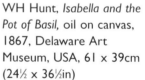

WH Hunt, *Isabella and the Pot of Basil,* oil on canvas, 1867, Delaware Art Museum, USA, 61 x 39cm (24½ x 36½in)

Hunt began this painting, based on Keats' poem *Isabella,* whilst he was in Florence in 1866. The Italian setting gave Hunt the opportunity to use an authentic set and employ a local model. The poem tells the story of Isabella, who is in mourning for her dead lover, Lorenzo. Lorenzo's head is in the jar of basil that Isabella is cradling and the grief-stricken girl feeds the plant with her tears. Hunt himself was to mourn the loss of his wife later that year.

DG Rossetti, *Joli Coeur*, oil on panel, 1867, Manchester City Art Gallery, UK, 38 x 30cm (15 x 12in)

This delightful painting has no pretext of a literary nature, unlike many of Rossetti's earlier pictures. The title refers to the heart-shaped necklace that the model is wearing, which is identifiable as the same one worn by one of the models in Rossetti's earlier painting *The Beloved*. The image is both sensuous and mildly erotic as the girl undoes her dress buttons to reveal the chemise beneath. The model's coquettish look adds to the eroticism of the picture.

JE Millais, *The Black Brunswicker,* watercolour, 1867, Whitworth Art Gallery, Manchester, UK, 38 x 30cm (15 x 12in)

This is a watercolour version of the image originally painted in 1860. However, Millais has sacrificed the background narrative detail for a close up of the couple. The polished death's head visible on the soldier's cap was a symbol of the Brunswickers, who were a fearsome fighting force. The group were instrumental in overcoming Napoleon, particularly at the battles of Quatre Bras and Waterloo, in which Napoleon was finally defeated.

DG Rossetti, *Venus Verticordia,* chalk on paper, 1867, private collection, 98 x 70cm (39½ x 27in)

This chalk drawing was a preliminary sketch for a large oil painting, and was modelled by Alexa Wilding. The title is taken from a Roman festival and refers to Venus as the 'changer of hearts'. At the festival, women washed the statue of the goddess and adorned her with flowers before contemplating their own relationships with men.

DG Rossetti, *Paolo and Francesca da Rimini,* watercolour, 1867, National Gallery of Victoria, Melbourne, Australia, 44 x 36cm (17½ x 14½in)

This image is taken from a section of a larger painting executed by Rossetti five years earlier. However, there are some differences between this and the original. The picture's frame is engraved with ivy, symbolic of immortality, and appended with text from Dante's *Inferno*. The story of Paolo and Francesca has been an inspiration for many artists, including Ingres, Cabanel and of course Rossetti, who was drawn to it by his interest in Dante.

Frederick Sandys, *Love's Shadow,* oil on panel, 1867, private collection, 41 x 32cm (16½ x 30¾in)

Sandys was living with Rossetti in Chelsea during 1866, and went on a long walking holiday with him in the autumn. It is easy to see in this work the influence that Rossetti had on him. In fact, Rossetti accused Sandys of plagiarism as a result of this painting and the friends fell out over it. The sitter is Mary Jones, who became Sandys' mistress, and with whom he had ten children.

Ford Madox Brown, *Romeo and Juliet,* watercolour, 1867, Whitworth Art Gallery, Manchester, UK, 48 x 33cm (46¼ x 13in)

The famous balcony scene, and its two protagonists from Shakespeare's play have been brought to life by Madox Brown in a riot of colour, set against the city of Verona. The black crows are a personification of hope, symbolizing the young lovers' wishes for the future. However, the presence of the rock rose in the foreground signified imminent death in Victorian times.

Ford Madox Brown, *The Nosegay,* watercolour, c.1867, Ashmolean Museum, Oxford, UK, 47 x 32cm (18¾ x 12¾in)

Like Millais, Madox Brown wanted to attract 'patrons who wanted something pretty'. This picture is one of two versions, both using his daughter Catherine as the model. By this time, Madox Brown was moving away from a strict Pre-Raphaelite aesthetic in favour of genre pictures and portraits. The 1860s and early 1870s were to be Madox Brown's most prosperous years.

E Burne-Jones, *Green Summer*, oil on canvas, 1868, private collection, 65 x 106cm (26 x 42½in)

Burne-Jones originally painted a watercolour version in 1864 of this later oil painting. The theme is heavily influenced by Venetian art, particularly Giorgione's *Fête*

Champêtre, which Burne-Jones would have admired on his visits to Italy. The title of the painting is taken from Sir Thomas Malory's collection of Arthurian legends, *Le Morte d'Arthur*. The picture was executed in the Abbey Woods in Kent, with Burne-Jones's wife and sisters acting as models.

DG Rossetti, *Lady Lilith*, oil on canvas, 1864–8, Delaware Art Museum, USA, 98 x 85cm (39¼ x 34in)

This painting was begun in 1864, the sitter being Fanny Cornforth. The work was commissioned by Frederick

Leyland and completed in 1868. However, Rossetti took the painting back again in 1872 when he reworked the face, this time substituting Alexa Wilding. Lilith is a Jewish mythological figure supposed to be the first wife of Adam.

DG Rossetti, *Mrs William Morris*, oil on canvas, 1868, Kelmscott Manor, Oxford, UK, 111 x 90cm (44 x 36in)

At the top of this painting is a Latin inscription, which translates as 'Famous for her husband, a poet, and most famous for her face; so let

this picture of mine add to her fame'. This indicates Rossetti's infatuation with Jane Morris at this time, and is also a very telling indictment of the subservience of women in this era. The portrait forms a double work with Rossetti's poem called *The Portrait*.

E Burne-Jones, *Hymenaeus,* oil on panel, 1868, Delaware Art Museum, USA, 83 x 56cm (33½ x 22½in)

Hymenaeus is the Greek god of marriage, and his name was also given to the songs that were sung during the bridal procession. The words 'hymen' and 'hymn' are both derived from the name Hymenaeus. Burne-Jones has managed to get both aspects of the god into this marriage scene. The artist's interest in the subject may have been induced by the start of his passionate relationship with Maria Zambaco at this time.

E Burne-Jones, *Sibylla Delphica,* oil on panel, 1868, Manchester Art Gallery, UK, 153 x 60cm (61½ x 24in)

The most famous incarnation of the Delphic Sybil is Michelangelo's version in the Sistine Chapel in Rome. Burne-Jones resurrects the theme, presenting his Sybil as an enchantress. In fact, the Delphic Sybil was a prophetess who practised her craft at the sacred Temple of Apollo at Delphi. She is said to have made prophesies pertaining to the outcome of the Trojan War.

Arthur Hughes, *The Pained Heart,* oil on canvas, 1868, private collection, 94 x 110cm (37½ x 44in)

This genre painting has little to do with a Pre-Raphaelite style, and is more in keeping with Millais' later work, which is often seen as an early form of Aestheticism. Hughes had become a purveyor of 'fancy' pictures, full of sentiment, and what Ruskin referred to as the 'pathetic fallacy'. However, Hughes added a notation on the back of the picture, 'Sigh no more, ladies', which is from Shakespeare's *Much Ado About Nothing,* a motif in line with Pre-Raphaelitism.

DG Rossetti, *Venus Verticordia,* oil on canvas, 1864–8, Russell Coates Art Gallery, Bournemouth, UK, 82 x 69cm (32½ x 27½in)

John Mitchell of Bradford commissioned this painting in 1864. Originally, the face was that of an unknown cook, but Rossetti subsequently reworked the painting with Alexa Wilding's face in 1867. The background is sumptuous with roses and honeysuckle, both symbols of love, as is the golden arrow Venus is holding. The Christian symbols of the halo around Venus's head and the butterfly, which normally denotes the Resurrection, are a mystery.

Ford Madox Brown,
My Native Land, Goodnight,
etching, 1869, private
collection, dimensions
unknown

Lord Byron's poem, *Adieu,
Adieu My Native Land* in
which he writes 'The night-
winds sigh, the breakers
roar', is the inspiration for
this etching by Madox
Brown, who had already
worked on an emigration
picture at sea – *The Last of
England.* Brown was later to
write mordantly about the
subject, 'The educated are
bound to their country by
quite other ties than the
illiterate man, whose chief
consideration is food and
physical comfort'.

Ford Madox Brown, *Emma
Madox Brown,* pastel, 1869,
Bolton Museum, UK,
77 x 53cm (30¾ x 21½in)

This delicate pastel portrait
is of the artist's wife, Emma,
at forty years old. By the
time this was executed,
Madox Brown had known
her as his model for over
twenty years. They married
in 1853, after his first wife
died, and between them
they had three children.
Although she was eight years
Madox Brown's junior, Emma
died in 1890, pre-deceasing
him by three years.

DG Rossetti, *Calliope Coronio*, 1869, private collection, 72 x 50cm (28½ x 20in)

Calliope Coronio was the sitter for this picture at the age of thirteen. She was the granddaughter of the great art collector and patron Alexander Ionides. He was part of a wealthy empire of importers and exporters, and his art patronage extended to Rossetti and Burne-Jones, as well as those of the Aesthetic Movement such as Whistler and George Frederick Watts. His daughter Aglaia, Calliope's mother, was also a friend and patron of Rossetti.

Ford Madox Brown, *Elijah Restoring the Widow's Son*, watercolour, 1868, Victoria and Albert Museum, London, 94 x 62cm (37½ x 25in)

In 1863 Madox Brown and several other Pre-Raphaelite artists were commissioned to provide illustrations for *The Bible Gallery*, a book published in 1881 by the Dalziel brothers. Madox Brown decided to make full-scale paintings from some of these drawings, including this one which tells the story of the prophet Elijah bringing a young boy back from the brink of dying.

DG Rossetti, *Pandora*, chalk on paper, 1869, Faringdon Collection, Oxford, UK, 101 x 73cm (40½ x 29¼in)

The model for this ethereal chalk drawing was Jane Morris. It marked the beginning of a very intense connection between Rossetti and Jane, although it is unclear whether their relationship was sexual. It is perhaps fitting that the subject of this work is Pandora. In the image she has already opened the box revealing all man's sins, closing it in time to retain only hope.

Ford Madox Brown, *The Finding of Don Juan by Haidee*, watercolour, 1869, National Gallery of Victoria, Melbourne, Australia, 48 x 58cm (19¼ x 23¼in)

The inspiration for the painting is Byron's epic poem, *Don Juan*, published in 1824. In the second canto of the poem, Don Juan, the infamous womanizer, has set sail from Cadiz but encounters a storm and is shipwrecked. Haidee and her maid Zoe find and take care of Don Juan, but the story ends tragically after she falls in love with him.

Ford Madox Brown, *I Due Foscari*, etching, 1869, private collection, 11 x 7cm (4½ x 2¾in)

Brown may well have seen the English premiere of Verdi's opera *I Due Foscari* in April 1847, which is based on Byron's play *The Two Foscari*. It is set in 15th-century Venice, and Jacopo Foscari has been convicted of murder. This picture depicts his wife visiting Jacopo in prison and embracing him before he is sent into exile without her for his crime.

WH Hunt, *Bianca*, oil on canvas, 1868–9, Worthing Museum, UK, dimensions unknown

While Hunt was in Florence in 1868 he began this painting, the model for which was an American woman, Miss Lydiard. While Hunt was undertaking the picture, he discussed the possibility of marriage with his new model. However, she was not prepared to go on a tour to the Holy Land with him, which made him reconsider his proposal. The picture has a strange mix of Italian and English influences.

DG Rossetti, *Beata Beatrix,* oil on canvas, 1864–70, Birmingham Museum and Art Gallery, UK, 87 x 61cm (34¾ x 24½in)

As a memorial piece to his late wife Lizzie, Rossetti began this painting from drawings he kept of her, describing the picture as a 'poetic work'. The politician William Cowper-Temple commissioned the painting, which was not completed until 1870. The frame contains a number of inscriptions including the date of Beatrice's death on the 9th June, 1290, suggesting that Rosetti still regarded Lizzie as his own incarnation of Beatrice.

E Burne-Jones, *Knights and the Briar Rose,* oil on canvas, 1869, private collection, 60 x 128cm (24 x 51in)

In 1869 Burne-Jones was troubled by the effectiveness of his art in terms of its transforming and cathartic powers for the viewer. He felt that for his work to be of any value, either politically or socially, the themes had to be understood in terms of the metaphysical. This painting is one of a series based on the story of Sleeping Beauty as an allegory of tenacity in the face of adversity.

DG Rossetti, *Christ Preaching,* stained glass, 1870, Christ Church, London, UK, dimensions unknown

This stained glass panel, one of a series designed by Rossetti and Morris, was installed in a neo-classical church that had been remodelled by William Butterfield in 1867 in the gothic revival style. The church counted Rossetti's sister Christina among its congregation. The panels collectively depict Christ's Sermon on the Mount.

E Burne-Jones, *Autumn,* gouache, 1869–70, private collection, 123 x 45cm (49 x 18in)

This is one of a series of four panels completed by Burne-Jones, known as the *Masque of the Four Seasons,* with each panel depicting a different season. The inspiration for the work came from William Morris's poem, *Lapse of the Year.* The artist has included a corresponding line from the poem at the foot of the pedestal on which the figure of Autumn is standing, 'Laden autumn here I stand'.

Color d'amore e di pietà sembianti

DG Rossetti, *The Lady of Pity,* pastel, 1870, Bradford Art Gallery, UK, 85 x 72cm (34 x 29in)

The motif of this painting has its origins in Dante's *Vita Nuova.* The title refers to the 'Lady of the window' who watches the heartbroken Dante mourning the loss of his beloved Beatrice. The model for this drawing was Jane Morris, who fulfilled a similar role in consoling Rossetti after the death of Lizzie. As Rossetti's affection for Jane grew, he also began to portray her as Beatrice.

E Burne-Jones, *Beatrice*, gouache, 1870, private collection, 67 x 49cm (26¾ x 19½in)

Maria Zambaco, Burne-Jones's mistress, modelled for this portrayal of Beatrice. She is seen carrying an olive branch, a symbol of peace. In the doorway are three onlookers, including the artist's wife Georgiana. They watch as Beatrice goes to meet Dante to take him on his journey through Purgatory toward Paradise, as related in *The Divine Comedy*.

E Burne-Jones, *The Evening Star*, gouache, 1870, private collection, 79 x 56cm (31½ x 22½in)

The title of this painting appears to be at odds with what it is depicting as, in Greek mythology, the Evening Star is a male figure, Hesperus, who represents Venus in the evening. His brother was Eosphorus, the Morning Star, and their mother was Eos, the goddess of the dawn. The artist appears to have conflated the legends and it is unclear what the figure is intended to represent.

DG Rossetti, *Jane Morris*, pencil, 1870, Kelmscott Manor, Oxford, UK, dimensions unknown

By 1870, when this drawing was completed, Rossetti had been corresponding with Jane Morris for some time. His letters had become increasingly affectionate, with one letter stating that 'no one else seems alive at all to me now, and places that are empty of you are empty of all life'.

E Burne-Jones, *King René's Wedding*, oil on canvas, 1870, private collection, dimensions unknown

Burne-Jones executed a number of images around this motif, including a cabinet panel and some stained glass designs in the early 1860s. He returned to the theme for this painting on canvas. René of Anjou was only ten years old when he married the nine-year old Isabel, a factor not considered in this picture, with the artist preferring to focus on medieval romanticism rather than accurate narrative.

DG Rossetti, *Woman with a Fan*, crayon, 1870, Birmingham Museum and Art Gallery, UK, 96 x 71cm, (38½ x 28½in)

The year this was drawn, Rossetti published his first book of poetry. Although most of the works had been published in magazines, this was his first compilation as a book. He had been suffering with his eyesight prior to this time, and had taken a break from painting in order to rest his eyes and concentrate on this new project. This work, executed in crayon, marks Rossetti's return to drawing and painting. The model is Fanny Cornforth.

JE Millais, *A Knight Errant,*
lithograph, 1870,
private collection,
dimensions unknown

This painting is notable for
being Millais' only full-length
female nude. In compliance
with Victorian mores, the
artist has set his nude within
the context of a
mythological or legendary
scene, similar to his earlier
Pre-Raphaelite works.
A coloured lithograph of the
work was made after Millais'
death as an illustration for a
book on chivalry.

DG Rossetti, *Sibylla Palifera,*
oil on canvas, 1865–70,
Lady Lever Art Gallery,
Liverpool, UK, 98 x 85cm
(39¼ x 34in)

A number of preliminary
drawings exist for this work,
begun in 1864 and featuring
Alexa Wilding as the model.
The banker George Rae,
one of Rossetti's patrons,
commissioned the work,
completed in 1870. Since the
figure is a sibyl, the reference
to the palm must be secular,
and denotes victory. There
are other symbolic
ambiguities in the picture,
including butterflies referring
to the soul and poppies that
denote sleep.

DG Rossetti, *Portrait of a Lady,* chalk on paper, 1870, private collection, 49 x 39cm (19½ x 15½in)

For many years this portrait was believed to be of Anglaia Coronio, the Greek heiress. However, recent scholarship has shown it is in fact Burne-Jones's model and one-time lover Maria Zambaco, who was in fact Anglaia's cousin. A comparison of portraits of the cousins reveals how the mistake was made, as they were very similar in looks.

DG Rossetti, *La Donna Della Fiamma,* pastel, 1870, Manchester Art Gallery, UK, 86 x 66cm (34½ x 26½in)

In mythology the flame is the personification of the goddess Venus, hence the term used in the context of a loved one. In the early 1870s Rossetti used Jane Morris in many sittings such as this, to portray the more abstract and contemplative aspects of an intimate love without using a literary pretext. The effect is enhanced by the ethereal effect of the medium.

E Burne-Jones, *Phyllis and Demophoön,* watercolour, 1870, Birmingham Museum and Art Gallery, 92 x 46cm (36¾ x 18½in)

When this picture was first exhibited at the Watercolour Society it caused outrage because of its depiction of full frontal male nudity.

Burne-Jones was deeply offended by the critical response to the picture, and withdrew all of his works from public exhibitions for several years. In a heated discussion with the president of the Society he refused to succumb to pressure and alter the picture, resigning as a member as a result.

DG Rossetti, *Silence*, black and red chalk, 1870, Brooklyn Museum, New York, USA, 106 x 77cm (42½ x 30¾in)

Jane Morris sat for this depiction of a woman holding a branch from a peach tree. During the Renaissance this symbol was used to denote the linking of the heart and the tongue, and came to represent truth that emanates from the union of both. The title is something of an irony, as Rossetti had been forthright about his feelings in his correspondence to Jane.

AESTHETIC PRE-RAPHAELITISM 1870–1880

During this decade, influences from other artists who emphasized aesthetic values over moral, social or political considerations in art changed the emphasis of pictorial values. They included Frederic Leighton, George Frederick Watts and JM Whistler, who were more interested in the decadence and symbolism of writers such as Théophile Gautier (1811–72) in France and Walter Pater (1839–94) in England, than in Tennyson and Keats. Aestheticism was also influenced by Japanese culture and had a marked effect on design culture as well. Of the Pre-Raphaelite painters, it profoundly affected the work of both Burne-Jones and Rossetti in particular.

Left: E Burne-Jones, Pan and Psyche, *oil on canvas, 1872–4, private collection, 60 x 53cm (24 x 21½in)*
Above: E Burne-Jones, Winter, *gouache, 1869–70, private collection, 123 x 45cm (49 x 18in)*

DG Rossetti, *Study for 'The Bower Meadow'*, 1871–2, Fitzwilliam Museum, Cambridge, UK, 80 × 67cm (37 × 26½in)

In 1871, Rossetti began making preliminary drawings and sketches for a major painting, *The Bower Meadow*. Some were executed as single figures and some, as here, were in a group. He also used a range of media to highlight or soften features. The model is Jane Morris, who appears to be sitting for both adult figures; the child is her daughter May.

DG Rossetti, *Study of a Female Nude*, pastel, 1870s, private collection, 76 × 61cm (30½ × 24½in)

The precise date for this drawing is not known, but an earlier version as a study for his picture *The Loving Cup* was executed in 1867. This image, however, seems to be richer in texture, as typified by his work of the early 1870s. The sitter is probably Ellen Smith, who was also used in watercolour replicas of the original oil painting.

Arthur Hughes, *Sir Galahad: Quest of the Holy Grail*, oil on canvas, 1870, Walker Art Gallery, Liverpool, UK, 113 x 168cm (45 x 67in)

Sir Galahad was the most esteemed of knights at the court of King Arthur, who, legend has it, was charged by God to seek the Holy Grail. His journey is perilous; often travelling alone he encounters many adversaries, but is always overseen by guardian angels. Hughes, one of the old-school Pre-Raphaelites, appears to have been inspired by Burne-Jones in his portrayal of the angels.

E Burne-Jones, *The March Marigold,* oil on canvas, 1870, private collection, dimensions unknown

The name *March Marigold* is possibly a derivation of the marsh marigold, common in the British Isles. In medieval times it was brought into church at Easter time as 'Mary's gold' in homage to the Virgin Mary, hence the suggestion it was picked in March. The flower is also referenced in Shakespeare's play *Cymbeline* as the 'winking marybuds'.

DG Rossetti, *Jenny Morris Aged 10*, pastel, 1871, Kelmscott Manor, Oxford, UK, 44 x 39cm (17½ x 15½in)

In 1871 Rossetti and William Morris took a joint lease on a house in Oxfordshire, Kelmscott Manor, as a retreat from London life. That year, Morris had decided to embark on a journey to Iceland, leaving his wife Jane and two children alone at the property with Rossetti, who decided to spend the summer there. Rossetti made several portraits of the Morrises, including this one of Jane (Jenny) Morris, at that time.

Ford Madox Brown, *The Corsair's Return,* watercolour, 1870–1, Delaware Art Museum, USA, 28 x 38cm (11 x 15in)

In medieval times, the corsair was a privateer authorized by the French king to raid enemy ships, steal their cargo and sell the goods to fund wars. Often they would be away from home for many months. This corsair has returned to find his lover in a deep sleep, as symbolized by the poppies strewn about her bed. The doves in the picture suggest her chastity in his absence.

DG Rossetti, *Dante's Dream,* oil on canvas, 1871, Walker Art Gallery, Liverpool, UK, 216 x 312cm (86¼ x 124½in)

Rossetti had painted a watercolour around this theme in 1856. This later reprisal of the motif is much larger, and the fact it is painted in oils suggests it was intended as a serious historical picture. The models too have changed from the earlier version, with Jane Morris replacing Annie Miller and Alexa Wilding and Marie Spartali making appearances. William Graham, Rossetti's patron, commissioned the painting.

DG Rossetti, *May Morris Aged 9,* pastel, 1871, Kelmscott Manor, Oxford, UK, 44 x 39cm (17½ x 15½in)

This is another of Rossetti's portraits of the Morris children that was undertaken while staying at Kelmscott Manor in the summer of 1871. This picture depicts Mary (May) Morris, the youngest daugter of William and Jane. May Morris learned to embroider as a young girl from her aunt, Bessie Burden. She then studied embroidery at the National Art Training School, later the Royal College of Art. Following this she became the director of embroidery at her father's business, where she became an inspiration and raised the level of the craft for subsequent generations.

DG Rossetti, *Proserpina*,
coloured chalk, 1871, The
Ashmolean Museum,
Oxford, UK, 22 x 11cm
(8¾ x 4½in)

This is a small study for a
large oil painting that
Rossetti undertook in the
mid-1870s of Proserpina,
goddess of the underworld.
The figure preoccupied
Rossetti for some time after,
and he made several
versions of the motif and
also wrote a sonnet around
the subject. The theme of
the underworld seems to
have fascinated Rossetti at
this time, perhaps borrowing
inspiration from Burne-Jones.

Ford Madox Brown, *Dream
of Sandanapalus,* tempera on
paper, 1871, Delaware Art
Museum, USA, 47 x 56cm
(18¾ x 22½in)

Inspired by Byron's poem
about Sardanapalus, Madox
Brown seems to have
misunderstood the legend of
the last king of Assyria in
much the same way as the
poet had done before him.
Byron was criticized for his
inaccurate portrayal of a
semi-fictional character. Far
from dreaming, Sardanapalus,
the last king of Assyria, was
forced to commit suicide after
his last line of defences
around his kingdom had failed.
The decadent king boxed
himself, as well as his eunuchs
and concubines, inside a great
funeral pyre and burned them
all to death.

E Burne-Jones, *The Sleeping Beauty*, gouache and watercolour, 1871, Manchester City Art Gallery, UK, 26 x 36cm (10½ x 14½in)

By the time of this picture, Burne-Jones had developed a mature style of painting that he summed up as 'a beautiful romantic dream of something that never was and never will be … in a land no one can define or remember, only desire'. This is a significant shift away from Ruskin's idea of 'truth to nature', and typifies the second wave of Pre-Raphaelitism that combines with aspects of Aestheticism. This image of the fairy-tale princess embodies this approach.

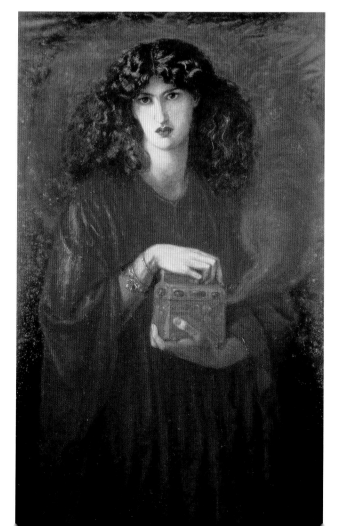

DG Rossetti, *Pandora*, oil on canvas, 1871, private collection, 128 x 77cm (51 x 30¾in)

Unusually, this picture was first exhibited in Glasgow. It was commissioned by the Academy artist John Graham, who later became Graham-Gilbert after marrying Jane Gilbert, a wealthy heiress who was native to Glasgow. Jane Gilbert was instrumental in setting up various arts institutions in Glasgow, including the Institute for Fine Arts, where this picture was first exhibited. Graham owned several Old Master Paintings.

Ford Madox Brown, *Jacob and Joseph's Coat,* oil on panel, 1871, private collection, 56 x 52cm (22½ x 21in)

The work Madox Brown undertook for 'The Firm' altered his painting style in the 1870s, seeing him return to historical narratives. In this painting Madox Brown depicts the Bible story of Jacob, who gave his favourite son, Joseph, a coat of many colours, making his other sons jealous. The brothers conspire to sell Joseph as a slave, and bring the coat back to Jacob covered in blood to trick him into believing that wild animals had killed Joseph.

DG Rossetti, *The Bower Meadow,* oil on canvas, 1871, Manchester City Art Gallery, UK, 83 x 62cm (33½ x 25in)

The background to this picture was begun in 1851 when he and Hunt spent time at Sevenoaks, in Kent. It was originally on a theme from Dante, but Rossetti took up the canvas again with a different mindset, this time to encapsulate the actual forces of love rather than a depiction of it based on a literary source. Unusually for this period, the sitters were Alexa Wilding and Marie Spartali rather than Rossetti's favourite, Jane Morris.

DG Rossetti, *Water Willow,* oil on canvas, 1871, Delaware Art Museum, USA, 33 x 27cm (13 x 10½in)

Several versions of this picture were executed between 1871 and 1873, but this is the only one painted in oils. It depicts Jane Morris holding a branch from a water willow, possibly from the grounds of Kelmscott, the manor house seen in the background. Rossetti had purchased the lease on this house in 1871 and spent that summer there.

Ford Madox Brown, *Convalescent,* coloured chalks, 1872, Birmingham Museum and Art Gallery, UK, 48 x 44cm (19½ x 17½)

In 1872, Madox Brown took it upon himself to care for Rossetti's business affairs after Rossetti had suffered a nervous breakdown. Unfortunately, Madox Brown was also unwell and suffering from gout. Matters came to a head when Madox Brown's wife, Emma, was struck down with a mystery illness and became bedridden. She is depicted here with a pale complexion holding a posy of pansies, which are symbolic of thoughtfulness. Emma died in 1890 after another long illness.

DG Rossetti, *May Morris*, 1872, private collection, dimensions unknown

Despite only being ten years of age at the time of this drawing, May Morris looks very sophisticated and womanly, and remarkably like her mother, Jane.

Princess Helena, the fifth child of Queen Victoria, was the founder of the Royal School of Needlework, which was set up in the same year as this picture was undertaken. Both William and May Morris were instrumental in helping to commercialize needlework as an industry.

DG Rossetti, *Veronica Veronese,* oil on canvas, 1872, Delaware Art Museum, USA, 105 x 86cm (42 x 34½in)

The sitter for this painting was Alexa Wilding, who borrowed the green dress from Jane Morris. The unusual title appears to be the artist paying homage to the 16th-century Venetian painter, Paolo Veronese, although Rossetti suggested it had the sound of a musical genius, alluded to by the inclusion of a violin in the picture. It was sold to Frederick Leyland.

Arthur Hughes, *Jack o' Lantern,* oil on canvas, 1872, private collection, dimensions unknown

Hughes's later career centred around book illustration, but occasionally he used a drawing to work up into a full painting, as in this example. This painting has its roots in an illustration Hughes produced for John Milton's *Comus.* In the painting, two children are looking toward the marshland, where they see a Jack o' lantern or will o' the wisp, a phenomenon resulting from the combustion of marsh gases that emits an eerie light.

Ford Madox Brown, *Cordelia's Portion,* watercolour, 1866–72, Lady Lever Art Gallery, Liverpool, UK, 71 x 107cm (28¼ x 43in)

Based on Shakespeare's *King Lear,* this is Madox Brown's last painting on this subject, although the play had fixated him since the 1840s. It is composed in intimate detail, akin to works from his early career, and depicts the opening scene of the play in which Lear disinherits Cordelia. The King of France offers her marriage with the words, 'Fairest Cordelia, thou art rich, being poor'.

DG Rossetti, *La Ghirlandata,*
oil on canvas, 1873,
Guildhall Art Gallery,
London, UK, 116 x 88cm
(56¼ x 35¼in)

William Graham paid £840
for this painting (about
£55,000 today) in 1873.
The title translates as the
'garlanded lady', and Alexa
Wilding modeled for the
lady, with May Morris for
both angel heads. Rossetti
wrote to William Bell Scott
in enthusiastic terms about
the work, which is of
'flowers and leaves all most
carefully done from nature',
a principle tenet of his
earlier work.

DG Rossetti, *Ligeia Siren,*
coloured chalks, 1873,
private collection,
42 x 34cm (16¾ x 13½in)

The sirens were mythological
creatures of the sea who
lured sailors to the deaths by
their music and song,
encouraging them to sail
their ships too close to the
rocky coastline. Stories vary
as to their numbers but the
consensus is that there were
only a few, the Ligeia being
one of them. Edgar Allen
Poe wrote a short story
based around the legend of
the Ligeia, which may well
have inspired Rossetti.

WH Hunt, *The Shadow of Death*, oil on canvas, 1870–3, Leeds Museum and Art Gallery, UK, 94 x 74cm (37½ x 29½in)

This is a smaller preliminary version of Hunt's later oil painting. Hunt created it at this size as he wanted to be able to take it around to different locations and carry out painting experiments. He took both versions with him on his return to Jerusalem and worked on them simultaneously. His diary refers to the considerable changes and corrections he made to both pictures, which explains the long gestation period of the painting.

E Burne-Jones, *Garden of the Hesperides*, oil on canvas, 1870–3, private collection, 114 x 77cm (45½ x 30¾in)

When the goddess Hera married Zeus, she was given a tree that bore golden apples, which granted immortality to those who ate them. The Hesperides were the guardians of the tree, but as Hera was untrusting of their loyalty, she placed a serpent called Ladon around the tree also. In this picture, the Hesperides are attempting to lure the snake away with their song in order that they can taste the fruit for themselves.

John Roddam Spencer Stanhope, *The Labours of Psyche,* tempera on panel, 1873, private collection, 79 x 31cm (31½ x 12½in)

These panels tell of the tasks set by Venus for Psyche, who has fallen in love with her son, Cupid. Venus is jealous of Psyche's beauty. The panel on the right tells of the most dangerous of the tasks, to obtain a casket containing beauty from Proserpine, the queen of the underworld. Psyche is eventually made immortal by Cupid.

E Burne-Jones, *Study for the Head of Nimue*, watercolour, Delaware Art Museum, USA, 76 x 51cm (30½ x 20½in)

This watercolour is a preparatory work for Burne-Jones's major work, *The Beguiling of Merlin*. He had already explored the theme in a large watercolour in 1861, but it was executed as an illustration of Arthurian legend. The later version has a more ethereal and transient quality, which is in line with the artist's Symbolist agenda. Nimue's dress has also changed dramatically in this version, to a more form-fitting Aesthetic style.

DG Rossetti, *Blanzifiore,* oil on canvas, 1873, private collection, 41 x 33cm (16½ x 13in)

The dominant symbolic feature of this picture is the bunch of snowdrops the woman holds in her hand, a reminder of the first flowers of early spring. The legendary snowdrop was the first flower to bloom after the Fall of Man, when Adam and Eve were driven from the Garden of Eden. making them symbolic of hope. Traditionally, snowdrops are the first flowers to be brought into church after Christmas, replacing images of the Virgin Mary during Candlemas.

DG Rossetti, *Study of Mrs William Morris,* pencil, c.1873, Fitzwilliam Museum, Cambridge, UK, 30 x 27cm (12 x 10½in)

Between 1871 and 1874, Rossetti executed a large number of sketches and finished drawings of Jane Morris and her two daughters at Kelmscott Manor. In between he had suffered a breakdown and attempted suicide. In 1873 he began the painting *Proserpine* using Jane as the model. As work was in progress he made a number of studies of a slightly more erotic or suggestive nature, as this sketch demonstrates.

E Burne-Jones, *Lot and his Daughters,* watercolour and chalk, 1874, Cecil Higgins Gallery, Bedford, UK, 76 x 59cm (30½ x 23½in)

In 1874 the Viceroy of India, Lord Mayo, was assassinated and plans were made to erect a memorial window to him at the cathedral in Calcutta. Burne-Jones, on behalf of Morris and Co, executed this design of *Lot and his Daughters*, who are fleeing Sodom. The figure on the left is Lot's wife, who has looked back to the burning city and is about to be turned into a pillar of salt.

DG Rossetti, *A Roman Widow,* oil on canvas, 1874, Museo de Arte de Ponce, Puerto Rico, 105 x 93cm (42 x 37½in)

Another in his series of Venetian-inspired beauties, this large oil painting was for Rossetti's patron Frederick Leyland. Two years after the completion of the painting, Leyland commissioned JM Whistler to execute a fabulous interior design that became known as 'The Peacock Room', an exemplar of the Anglo-Japanese style that heralded the Aesthetic Movement.

Ford Madox Brown, *Byron's Dream,* oil on canvas, 1874, Manchester Art Gallery, UK, 72 x 55cm (28½ x 22in)

Edward Moxon published a new edition of Byron's poetic works in 1870. The frontispiece contained an illustration by Madox Brown, which is essentially a vignette of this painting that was executed in 1874. The painting is an interpretation of the poem *The Dream* written in 1816, that posits the writer overlooking the Misk Hills in England, the location of his ancestral home.

DG Rossetti, *Study for the Figure of Love,* red crayon, 1874, private collection, 58 x 37cm (23¼ x 14¾)

The central figure in Rossetti's painting *Dante's Dream* from 1871 was the figure of Love personified. The artist had made one previous version of the painting in 1856, and was to make a perfected large-scale version in 1880. En route, Rossetti made a number of drawings in different media, including this one, and another the same year showing Love kissing Beatrice.

DG Rossetti, *Marigolds*, oil on canvas, 1874, Nottingham Castle Museum and Art Gallery, 114 x 74cm (45½ x 29½in)

It is suggested that the model for this painting was 'Little Annie', a maid who was working at Kelmscott Manor at the time it was produced. The scene is set in late winter, and the girl has returned from the garden where she has picked marsh marigolds to display on the mantelpiece. The occasional table next to the fire picks up the reflections from the flames, and a cat is playing with a ball of wool.

E Burne-Jones, *William Morris Working on a Tapestry*, pencil, date unknown, Fitzwilliam Museum, Cambridge, UK, 14 x 9cm (5½ x 3½in)

Despite the intensity of industry generated by William Morris's design company, there were lighter moments for artists working with him. Both Rossetti and Burne-Jones enjoyed producing these cartoons, some of which were ribald and often featured Morris as the butt of the jibe. Morris had been interested in tapestry from his earliest attempts at reproducing medieval wall hangings in 1856.

Ford Madox Brown, *Cromwell on his Farm,* oil on canvas, 1873–4, Walker Art Gallery, Liverpool, UK, 143 x 104cm (57¼ x 41½in)

The original oil sketch for this work was executed in 1853, and twenty years later Madox Brown painted this large-scale version. The painting depicts Oliver Cromwell overseeing work on his farm in the period just before he became a national figure during the English Civil War. The picture is contemplative in nature, with Cromwell preoccupied with his thoughts on the state of the country and monarchy, despite the activity surrounding him.

E Burne-Jones, *The Beguiling of Merlin,* oil on canvas, 1870–4, Lady Lever Art Gallery, Liverpool, UK, 186 x 111cm (74½ x 44½in)

Commissioned by Frederick Leyland, this painting took four years to complete. This depiction of Merlin's infatuation with Nimue, and its tragic consequences, is perhaps based on his own passionate affair with Maria Zambaco. Merlin's passion is clearly visible in the painting and his eyes are locked on the seductress. The decadent writer Oscar Wilde described the picture as 'full of magic'.

E Burne-Jones, *The Sirens*, pastel, c.1875, The South African National Gallery, Cape Town, South Africa, dimensions unknown

Burne-Jones has created an alternative worldliness in this dark foreboding place where sailors are lured onto the rocks by the beguiling sirens. The artist has used the motif of the sirens but has eschewed literary pretext to create a fantasy world that is frightening and compelling to view. The muted colours seem to anticipate the murky worlds depicted in 20th-century modernism, as typified by Picasso's Blue Period.

Ford Madox Brown, *May Memories,* oil on canvas, 1869–84, private collection, 43 x 30cm (17¼ x 12in)

This painting is of Madox Brown's second wife, Emma, and is both a portrait and a reflective piece. It is signed and dated '69–84' emphasizing the fact that it had an extraordinarily long gestation period. Emma is completely absorbed into the landscape, Madox Brown hardly differentiating between the tree and her hair. The pose is rather awkward and seems designed to emphasize her womanly disposition rather than the traditional Pre-Raphaelite depiction of the 'stunner'.

E Burne-Jones, *Laus Veneris*, oil on canvas, 1873–5, Laing Art Gallery, Newcastle upon Tyne, UK, 122 x 183cm (49 x 73in)

Thomas Carlyle's *German Romance* of 1827 brought the legends of European medievalism to the United Kingdom. The Brothers were inspired by these tales, especially those relating to the knight and poet Tannhäuser, who, legend has it, discovered the Venusberg, the underground home of Venus. Algernon Swinburne wrote his poem *Laus Veneris*, around this theme, which in turn inspired this painting.

Ford Madox Brown, *Cordelia's Portion*, oil on canvas, 1867–75, Southampton Art Gallery, UK, 80 x 112cm (32 x 44½in)

After completing the first version of this picture in watercolour, Madox Brown was commissioned by a new patron, Albert Wood, to remake it in oil. It took eight years to complete, as the artist was working on many different pictures in this, his most financially lucrative, period. His son Oliver may well have helped in the execution of this painting before he tragically died in 1874.

DG Rossetti, *La Bella Mano,*
oil on canvas, 1875,
Delaware Art Museum, USA,
163 x 117cm (65½ x 46½in)

Both May Morris and Alexa
Wilding sat for this painting,
which is an exploration of
both the physical and
spiritual manifestations of
love. Rossetti believed that
this combination creates the
perfect love of the soul, as
symbolized in Dante's
love for Beatrice. At the
time of its creation, Rossetti
wrote a sonnet to
accompany the work in
which he refers to the 'lips
of music measured speech'.

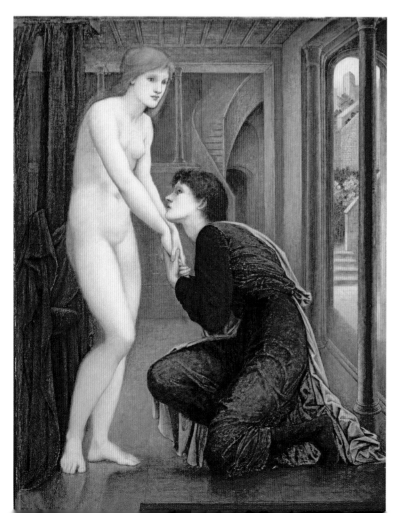

E Burne-Jones, *The Soul
Attains,* oil on canvas,
1875–8, private collection,
66 x 51cm (26½ x 20½in)

In 1875 Burne-Jones began
the *Pygmalion and the Image*
series of four pictures based
on Ovid's *Metamorphoses.*
This picture depicts
Pygmalion, a mythical king
who sculpted a statue that
was so beautiful he fell in
love with it. Venus took pity
on him and brought the
marble statue to life.
Burne-Jones appreciated the
allegorical meaning of the
story that transcends the
difference between
imagination and action.

JE Millais, *The Sound of Many Waters,* oil on canvas, 1876, The National Trust for Scotland, Fyvie Castle, UK, 148 x 214cm (59¼ x 85½in)

The subject of this painting is similar to a portrait of Ruskin that Millais had painted twenty years before. Millais has been faithful to nature in the waterfall and rock detail, but this painting lacks the slavish imitation of the minutiae found in his earlier Pre-Raphaelite works. It was shown at the Academy of 1877 and sold to a wool merchant, David Price, for £3,000 (over £200,000 today).

DG Rossetti, *Death of Lady Macbeth,* pen and ink, c.1875, The Ashmolean Museum, Oxford, UK, 31 x 36cm (30½ x 14½in)

Similarities can be drawn between the fictional Lady Macbeth and Rossetti in terms of their respective anxieties. Rossetti became addicted to chloral, which was used to treat insomnia but also induced a hypnotic state. Lady Macbeth's delirium was provoked by her guilt at the part she played in the murder of King Duncan. Rossetti was also guilt-ridden after the death of Lizzie, feeling that he too was responsible.

Simeon Solomon, *Night,* watercolour, ink and bodycolour, 1890, Royal Albert Memorial Museum, Exeter, UK, dimensions unknown

Solomon led a clandestine life after 1873, when he was arrested for lewd sexual acts in a public urinal. Two years previously, he published his prose poem *A Vision of Love Revealed in Sleep*, that dealt with sexual desires, justified through ancient Jewish and Christian writings. This picture of a Medusa-like creature, part woman and part animal, anticipates the arrival of the Symbolist Movement, and artists such as Fernand Khnopff, a decade later.

DG Rossetti, *Study for 'The Blessed Damozel'*, chalk on paper, 1876, Manchester City Art Gallery, UK, 55 x 57cm (22 x 22¾in)

William Graham commissioned Rossetti to paint *The Blessed Damozel* in 1871, but the artist did not begin the work until 1875, starting with a series of drawings, including this one. The sitter was Alexa Wilding, although Rossetti's intention was not to capture a portrait likeness, but rather to portray an embodiment of beauty and love.

WH Hunt, *Talking-whispering in the Synagogue, Full of Noisy People*, pen and ink, c.1876, private collection, 15 x 14cm (6 x 5½in)

There is no record of this drawing being used as a study for a larger picture, and one assumes therefore it was executed simply for the joy of drawing. It was drawn during Hunt's third visit to the Holy Land between 1875 and 1878. He seems to have been pleased with the outcome, as it is referred to in his autobiography and stayed in the family long after his death in 1910.

WH Hunt, *Triumph of the Innocents*, oil on canvas, 1876–87, Walker Art Gallery, Liverpool, UK, 158 x 248cm (63¼ x 99¼in)

Hunt has not been true to nature in depicting this scene. Instead he has separated the fidelity of the foreground and created a starry-skied backdrop. The attention to detail of the group is astounding, but Hunt has chosen to bathe them in an unnatural light.

Ford Madox Brown,
Self-portrait,
oil on canvas, 1877,
Fogg Art Museum, USA,
76 x 64cm (30½ x 25½in)

This self-assured pose of the artist is also a melancholic portrait. It was given as a gift to the writer Theodore Watts-Dunton, possibly in return for the kindnesses shown by him to Madox Brown's friends and fellow artists, including Rossetti during his breakdown and Algernon Swinburne, whom he helped to overcome alcoholism. Madox Brown too was a generous and kindly man, and he had an open-house policy during his affluent years of the 1870s.

Ford Madox Brown, *Jesus Washing Peter's Feet,* oil on canvas, 1876, Manchester Art Gallery, UK, 49 x 55cm (19½ x 22in)

The businessman and social reformer, Charles Rowley, commissioned this painting. It was the second version of the work, which had been heavily criticized in 1852 at the Academy, mainly because it depicted Jesus naked. The work was subsequently over-painted. In this version, Madox Brown returns to his original scheme but with Jesus semi-clad to appease his critics.

E Burne-Jones, *Days of Creation, (Fifth Day)*, gouache, 1870–6, Fogg Art Museum, USA, 102 x 36cm (40¾ x 14½in)

A scheme of six panels (framed as one picture) depicting the days of the Creation was commissioned by one of Burne-Jones's loyal patrons, William Graham, a Scottish liberal member of parliament. This one shows the fifth day, in which God commanded that the 'sea and the sky should be filled with living creatures', as symbolized by the seashells in the foreground, and the feather dresses the angels are wearing.

DG Rossetti, *Astarte Syriaca*, oil on canvas, 1877, Manchester Art Gallery, UK, 49 x 55cm (19½ x 22in)

The epitome of the femme-fatale, Rossetti's figure is a combination of Venus, the classical goddess of love, and Astarte, a Middle Eastern goddess of sexuality and war. She adopts a traditional 'pudica' pose that draws the viewer to the prominent breast and genital area, and yet her girdle, made of roses and pomegranates, symbolizes love and chastity.

DG Rossetti, *Mary Magdalene,* oil on canvas, 1877, Delaware Art Museum, USA, 78 x 66cm (31¼ x 26½in)

The much-maligned Mary Magdalene, who is proffered as a repentant prostitute in many pictures, is seen here as the true disciple of Jesus who was present at the crucifixion and at his burial. Rossetti depicts her as the model of sacred femininity; she holds a pomegranate, a symbol of her chastity, and is set against a background of passion-flowers, to signify Christ's own Passion on the cross.

E Burne-Jones, *The Cumaean Sibyl,* oil on panel, 1877, private collection, 153 x 60cm (61½ x 24in)

The influence of other artists showing at the new Grosvenor Gallery at this time is evident in this work. The group share the same style of Aestheticism and a preoccupation with other-worldly beings draped in comparatively plain dresses with long puffed sleeves. This style of 'artistic dress' became popular in intellectual, as well as artistic, circles in the last quarter of the nineteenth century.

DG Rossetti, *A Sea Spell,* oil on canvas, 1875–7, Fogg Art Museum, USA, 112 x 93cm (44½ x 37¼in)

Rossetti's biographer, Evelyn Waugh, speaks very unkindly of this painting, dismissing it as a 'work of a prematurely faltering mind'. This may in fact be true, but the work retains a delicate touch even if some of the symbolic elements are ambiguous. The sitter was Alexa Wilding, and it was painted at Broadstairs in Kent, the country home of the art collector, Frederick Leyland, who purchased the painting.

John Roddam Spencer Stanhope, *Eve Tempted,* tempera on panel, c.1877, Manchester City Art Gallery, UK, 49 x 55cm (19½ x 22in)

Stanhope loved Florence, and spent much of his life there absorbing and being influenced by the city's art. This work is painted in tempera, a traditional medium used by the *quattrocento* artists such as Piero della Francesca. The figure of Eve also evokes Florentine art, but the serpent is inspired by Burne-Jones, who acted as Stanhope's mentor despite being the younger of the two.

DG Rossetti, *Frederick Leyland*, pastel, 1879, The Wilmington Society of Fine Arts, Delaware, USA, 46 x 39cm (18½ x 15½in)

Fanny Cornforth owned this painting of one of the great art patrons of the 19th century, Frederick Leyland. Leyland was depicted in

Theodore Watts-Dunton's novel *Aylwin* as an elegantly dressed dandy, but in real life he was a ruthless businessman, liked by few people. He also had a reputation as a womanizer, and had two illegitimate children by a mistress with whom he lived until the end of his life in 1892.

E Burne-Jones, *The Mirror of Venus,* oil on canvas, 1870–6, private collection, 79 x122cm (31½ x 49in)

This is the earlier of two versions of this picture, which was exhibited at the newly opened Grosvenor Gallery in London to great acclaim. The image successfully blends a

Botticellian Venus with Aesthetic maidens but, unusually for Burne-Jones, the setting in an Arcadian landscape creates a lack of the dynamism that is often found in his work. The writer Henry James revered Burne-Jones's oeuvre, praising his 'fertility of invention' and 'remarkable gifts as a colourist'.

DG Rossetti, *Bruna Brunelleschi,* gouache, 1878, Fitzwilliam Museum, Cambridge, UK, 34 x 31cm (13½ x 12½in)

In a letter dated February 1878, Rossetti wrote to Jane Morris about this picture modelled on her. It bears a resemblance to one made ten years before, and Rossetti was keen that this image should not simply be seen as a repeat of his earlier work. In the letter he explained why he intended therefore to call it *Bruna Brunelleschi* as a reference to a fictional character who has brunette hair.

DG Rossetti, *The Blessed Damozel,* oil on canvas, 1875–8, Fogg Art Museum, USA, 137 x 97cm (54½ x 38¾in)

Rossetti's patron, William Graham, requested that the artist add a predella containing a smaller narrative appendage to the main picture. It was common practice in medieval and early Renaissance altarpieces to add predellas containing biblical narratives in a style that did not need to conform to hierarchical protocols. The figure beneath the 'damozel' is her waiting lover, lying in a pastoral landscape.

DG Rossetti, *La Donna Della Finestra,* oil on canvas, 1879, Fogg Art Museum, USA, 101 x 74cm (40½ x 29½in)

The title of this work translates as 'the lady of pity', and the figure was modeled by Jane Morris. Lines from Dante's *Vita Nuova* are appended to the frame of this picture: 'Mine eyes behold the blessed pity spring … and I become afraid that thou shouldst see my weeping and account it a base thing'. Frederick Ellis, an antiquarian bookseller who helped Morris set up his Kelmscott Press, purchased the painting.

Ford Madox Brown, *Tell's Son,* oil on canvas, 1880, private collection, 41 x 37cm (16½ x 14¾in)

The legend of William Tell was popularized in Europe after Rossini's opera, written around the legend, was performed in 1829. Madox Brown's picture shows Tell's son proudly displaying the apple after his father had shot it through with an arrow. The model for the painting was Madox Brown's grandson, Ford Madox Hueffer, who later wrote his grandfather's biography.

E Burne-Jones, *The Golden Stairs,* oil on canvas, 1876–80, Tate Gallery, London, UK, 269 x 117cm (67½ x 46½in)

There has been much debate about the meaning of this much-admired and surprisingly modern painting. The girls endlessly winding their way down the staircase imbue the work with a dreamlike quality that has inspired many artists, including Picasso, who is known to have admired Burne-Jones's work.

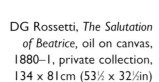

DG Rossetti, *The Salutation of Beatrice,* oil on canvas, 1880–1, private collection, 134 x 81cm (53½ x 32½in)

Unlike Rossetti's previous compositions of Beatrice, the figures of Dante and 'Love', who is protecting him, are consigned to the background so that the viewer is compelled to look only at her. She is walking in a street in Florence, past a rose bush on one side and some jasmine on the other. This was one of Rossetti's last paintings and was on his studio easel at the time of his death.

E Burne-Jones, *The Mill,* oil on canvas, 1870–80, Victoria and Albert Museum, London, UK, 91 x 198cm (36½ x 79¼in)

Constantine Ionides commissioned this painting in 1870, and the 'Three Graces' are modelled by members of his family; Marie Spartali, Aglaia

Coronio and Maria Zambaco. The original 'Three Graces' were daughters of Zeus and companions to the Muses, representing youth, mirth

and elegance. Since the Renaissance many artists have portrayed them interacting and dancing, but Burne-Jones brought a new spirituality to the scene.

E Burne-Jones, *Love That Moves the Sun,* watercolour, c.1880, private collection, 217 x 107cm (86½ x 43in)

This is a coloured version of a cartoon for a tapestry design by Burne-Jones. The embroiderer of the tapestry was Frances Graham, the daughter of his patron William. Burne-Jones fell in love with her and was hurt when she rebuffed him to marry another man. Nevertheless, they remained good friends, and Frances became his companion toward the end of his life.

DG Rossetti, *Mnemosyne*, oil on canvas, 1881, Delaware Art Museum, USA, 126 x 61cm (50½ x 24½in)

In Greek mythology Mnemosyne was the personification of memory. She slept with Zeus on nine consecutive nights, creating the nine Muses in the process. The painting is very similar in design to his *Astarte Syriaca*, and Rossetti penned some lines to accompany the picture: 'Thou fill'st from the winged chalice of the soul, Thy lamp, O Memory, fire-winged to its goal'.

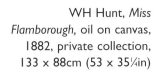

WH Hunt, *Miss Flamborough,* oil on canvas, 1882, private collection, 133 x 88cm (53 x 35¼in)

Hunt exhibited this painting at the Grosvenor Gallery in 1882. It is a portrait of his daughter Gladys in the pose of Miss Flamborough, a character from Oliver Goldsmith's novel *The Vicar of Wakefield*. Like Millais, Hunt was enchanted by the innocent beauty of young girls, a feature that is brilliantly portrayed in this painting, with all the credentials of true Pre-Raphaelitism.

THE FINAL YEARS, AFTER 1890

In the last twenty years of the century, Burne-Jones dominated Pre-Raphaelitism, Rossetti having died in 1882. However, other disciples of the aesthetic, such as John William Waterhouse and Evelyn de Morgan, joined its ranks for one last flowering of what came to be regarded as the high point of Victorian England, the most radical art movement in the country for three hundred years.

Left: E Burne-Jones, The Rock of Doom, *chalk, c.1880, private collection, 27 x 15cm (10½ x 6in)*
Above: E Burne-Jones, Design for 'The Sirens', *gouache and watercolour, 1890s, private collection, 51 x 70cm (20½ x 27¾in)*

E Burne-Jones, *Portrait of Marie Spartali,* oil on canvas, c. 19th century, private collection, 69 x 48cm (27 x 19in)

Apart from being a model for Burne-Jones and Rossetti, Marie Spartali was an accomplished Pre-Raphaelite artist in her own right. Ford Madox Brown taught her painting at the same time that he was teaching his own children. In 1871 she married an American journalist, William Stillman, and later travelled and worked as an artist in the USA. The inspiration for this picture is from one of Rossetti's poems.

E Burne-Jones, *Study for 'The Sleeping Princess',* oil on canvas, c.1881, private collection, 51 x 51cm (20½ x 20½in)

This sketch forms part of a large number of preliminary works for his *Briar Rose* series, which focus on the sleeping beauty legend. He had begun the cycle of paintings in 1871, inspired by Tennyson's poem *The Day-Dream,* which centred around the fairy tale. The Burne-Jones series was not intended as a narrative of the fairy tale but as an exploration of the power of love to overcome adversity.

E Burne-Jones, *The Tree of Forgiveness,* oil on canvas, 1881–2, Lady Lever Art Gallery, Liverpool, UK, 191 x 107cm (76½ x 42½in)

Perhaps in defiance of the critics of his *Phyllis and Demophoön*, Burne-Jones reprised the subject and the composition in this picture, carefully avoiding the full nudity that caused the previous criticism. Demophoön has returned to marry Phyllis, only to find that her fears that he will not return have driven her to suicide. The gods have turned her into an almond tree, but when the penitent Demophoön embraces the tree it turns back into the form of his lover.

DG Rossetti, *Proserpine,* oil on canvas, 1882, private collection, dimensions unknown

There are eight versions of this painting, some of which were not completed before the artist's death in 1882. The figure, modeled by Jane Morris, is of Proserpine, who was abducted by Pluto and became the Queen of the Underworld. When she was abducted, she ate four seeds from a pomegranate that belonged to Pluto, and from then on was forced to spend the four months of each year as his captive.

E Burne-Jones, *The Finding of Medusa,* gouache, 1882, Southampton Art Gallery, UK, 153 x 137cm (61½ x 54¾in)

Another from the *Perseus* series; this incomplete painting shows Perseus entering the cave where he encounters Medusa. He is seen using a mirror to locate her, to ensure that he does not look at her directly and get turned to stone. He is also wearing the helmet of invisibility so that when he beheads her she cannot locate him, before he places her head in the sack he is carrying.

Ford Madox Brown, *Madeline Scott,* oil on canvas, 1883, Manchester City Art Gallery, UK, 122 x 79cm (48¾ x 31½in)

At the end of his career, Madox Brown was occupied with the *Manchester Murals* series that he was undertaking for the new town hall. To undertake this large commission he relocated to Manchester, and took the opportunity to paint a number of portraits of its citizens, including this charming portrait of Madeline Scott, riding a tricycle. She was the daughter of CP Scott, the editor of the *Manchester Guardian* newspaper.

E Burne-Jones, *The Wheel of Fortune,* oil on canvas, 1875–83, Musée d'Orsay, Paris, France, 199 x 100cm (79½ x 40in)

The figures revolving around the Wheel of Life in this painting are clearly inspired by Michaelangelo's depictions of the male nude. Lady Fortune revolves the wheel, while the figures strapped to it are helpless to control their fate. One figure holds a golden arrow, suggesting that he has been selected for good fortune in life. This painting is essentially part of the Aesthetic movement, and yet retains a function, to remind the viewer that 'we take our turn at it (the wheel of fortune) and are broken upon it'.

E Burne-Jones, *The Doom Fulfilled,* gouache, 1882, Southampton Art Gallery, UK, 154 x 138cm (61¾ x 55in)

Begun in 1875 for the politician, and later Prime Minister, Arthur Balfour, who was also a great patron of the arts, the *Perseus* series of ten pictures took ten years to complete. The series is based on William Morris's poem *The Doom of King Acrisius,* although the antecedents for these mixed tales of Greek myth are to be found in the Renaissance paintings of Rubens and Titian.

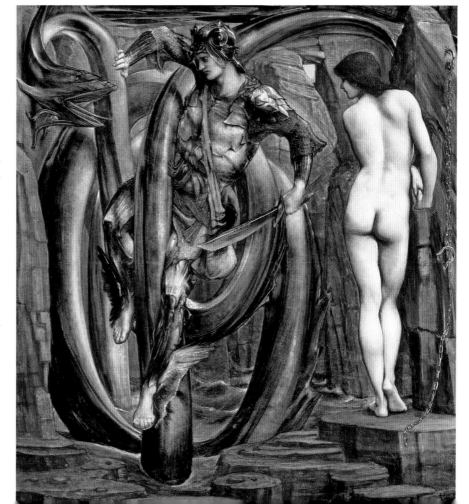

E Burne-Jones, *King Cophetua and the Beggar Maid*, oil on canvas, 1880-4, Tate Gallery, London, UK, 293 x136cm (117¼ x 54½in)

Frances Graham, the subject of Burne-Jones's unrequited love, modelled for the beggar maid in this painting, and the artist has accordingly placed some richly coloured anemones around the figure, a symbol of rejected love. The story, an Elizabethan folk tale, recounted by Tennyson, tells of a King who rejects courtly love until he meets a beggar whose beauty captivates him.

WH Hunt, *Amaryllis*, oil on panel, 1886, private collection, 64 x 53cm (25½ x 21½in)

Unlike Millais, Hunt had not been elected to the Academy, yet he still pursued the same line of 'fancy' pictures which would have suited their patrons. Instead, like Burne-Jones, he was drawn into the circle of exhibitors who showed at the Grosvenor Gallery, despite his pictures being at odds with the others in their pursuit of Aestheticism.

JW Waterhouse, *The Lady of Shalott,* oil on canvas, 1884, Tate Gallery, London, UK, 153 x 200cm (61½ x 80in)

One of the most visually popular pictures at the Tate Gallery, this was purchased by Sir Henry Tate and became part of his bequest. This large-scale painting is based on Tennyson's poem of the same name, in which the 'Lady' is paying the ultimate price for looking directly at Sir Lancelot. In this scene she is in the boat that will take her to her final resting place.

E Burne-Jones, *Alleluia,* tapestry, c.1885, Harris Museum, Preston, UK, 175 x 95cm (70 x 38in)

This is a design for a tapestry executed by Morris and Co, by whom Burne-Jones unlike the other Pre-Raphaelites, was retained after the company's restructure in 1875. His output was phenomenal, particularly as he was painting large-scale works as well, and involved stained glass and tapestry designs, mainly for ecclesiastical use. Burne-Jones was also involved in graphic designs for Morris's venture, the Kelmscott Press.

E Burne-Jones, *Danäe, or, The Tower of Brass,* oil on canvas, 1887–8, Glasgow Art Gallery, UK, 231 x 113cm (92½ x 45in)

Danäe was the subject of several amorous paintings from the Renaissance; Titian, for example, depicting her in a series of paintings as being lured by Cupid, and Rembrandt recalling the bedroom scene when she is being seduced by Zeus disguised as a shower of gold. Burne-Jones's image is one of contemplation as Danäe considers her imprisonment in a tower of brass, an attempt by her father to prevent her pregnancy.

WH Hunt, *Hercules in the Garden of the Hesperides,* painted plaster, 1887, Manchester City Art Gallery, UK, oval 69 x 52cm (27½ x 21in)

This painted plaster image of Hercules was made for Hunt to include as a prop in his painting *The Lady of Shalott.* The original oval was of Christ in majesty, which rather conflicts with the image from Arthurian legend. However this image bears little relationship to the demise of the 'Lady', except to reinforce the idea that no one is immortal.

WH Hunt, *Christ Among the Doctors,* oil on canvas, 1887, New Walk Museum, Leicester, UK, 64 x 126cm (25¾ x 50½in)

Hunt revisits the biblical narrative explored in his earlier painting *The Finding of the Saviour in the Temple* in this painting. The passage from Luke's Gospel that both of the paintings are based on has been visualised by several artists, such as in Albrecht Durer's *Christ Among the Doctors* (1506), and Hunt's contemporary Heinrich Hoffman's *Christ in the Temple.*

E Burne-Jones, *The Baleful Head*, oil on canvas, 1887, Staatsgalerie, Stuttgart, Germany, 155 x 130cm (62½ x 52in)

The original version of this painting was in gouache, and formed part of the *Perseus* series commissioned by Arthur Balfour. The painting depicts Perseus showing Andromeda how to view Medusa's head as a reflection, thus avoiding being turned to stone. The background has a classical feel and is probably inspired by the Renaissance landscapes that Burne-Jones had admired on his trips to Italy.

E Burne-Jones, *Angels of Creation,* stained glass, c.1890, Manchester College, Oxford, UK, dimensions unknown

The origins of Manchester College date to the late eighteenth century, where it was first homed in York, London and Manchester before finding its permanent home in a purpose-built property in Oxford in 1893. The building was designed by the gothic architect Thomas Worthington and incorporated exquisite detailing, such as this stained glass design by Burne-Jones.

Ford Madox Brown, *Crabtree Watching the Transit of Venus in 1639*, 1881–3, Manchester City Art Gallery, UK, 26 x 56cm (10½ x 22½in)

Madox Brown believed that he was underpaid for his murals at Manchester Town Hall. To supplement his income he painted several reduced versions, including this one. This scene depicts a local draper who observed Venus passing across the sun, the image reflecting in his telescope in a darkened room.

Evelyn de Morgan, *The Angel of Death,* oil on canvas, 1890, De Morgan Centre, London, UK, 124 x 93cm (49½ x 37½in)

Evelyn de Morgan was a prolific painter in the Pre-Raphaelite style. Her uncle was John Roddam Spencer Stanhope, who often invited her out to Florence where he lived. She was passionate about art from an early age and was greatly inspired by Florentine art, Botticelli being a particular favourite. She was married to the ceramicist William de Morgan.

E Burne-Jones, *The Failure of Sir Lancelot,* gouache, c.1890, private collection, dimensions unknown

Sir Lancelot slumps to the floor in disappointed slumber, having failed in his quest to find the Holy Grail. The Grail is subsequently found by Sir Galahad, Lancelot's illegitimate son, but Lancelot is only allowed a glimpse because he is an adulterer and cannot touch it. The design was for one of several huge tapestries for the newly rebuilt Stanmore Hall.

JW Waterhouse, *Circe Offering the Cup to Ulysses,* oil on canvas, 1891, Oldham Gallery, UK, 146 x 90cm (58½ x 36in)

Circe features in Homer's *Odyssey* as the daughter of Helios, the sun god. She lives on a remote island and her palace is surrounded by a dense forest inhabited by wild animals. She is proficient at making herbal potions, using them to tame the creatures that occupy the forest, but also to drug lost sailors. In this scene she is about to offer Odysseus one of her potions, but he has been warned of her guile.

E Burne-Jones, *The Council Chamber,* oil on canvas, 1872–92, Delaware Art Museum, USA, 124 x 264cm (49½ x 105½in)

This scene from *Sleeping Beauty* depicts the royal court, with the King on his throne, deep in an enchanted sleep and powerless to help the cursed Princess. Burne-Jones has used the branches that threaten to wrap themselves around the sleeping bodies to enhance the arabesque lines of the human forms.

Ford Madox Brown, *Dalton Collecting Marsh Fire Gas,* wall mural, 1879–93, Manchester Town Hall, UK, dimensions unknown

This panel is one of twelve that Brown was working on up until his death, each one telling part of the story of Manchester's history. They were commissioned to occupy the walls of the newly opened town hall, which was built in a neo-gothic style. This panel depicts the chemist John Dalton (1766–1844) collecting marsh gas for his experiments, leading to his radical theory that gases under extremes of pressure or temperature could be made into liquids.

WH Hunt, *The Miracle of the Sacred Fire,* oil on canvas, 1892–9, Fogg Art Museum, USA, 92 x 116cm (36¾ x 46¼in)

In the spirit of the painter and social critic William Hogarth, a hero to the early Pre-Raphaelites, Hunt painted this picture to satirize an event he saw while in the Holy Land. An Easter ritual saw the arrival of pilgrims in Jerusalem to witness the 'miracle' of a candle produced by an Orthodox Greek priest. The candle had apparently been lit by divine means and Hunt has depicted the farcical passing of the candle among the congregation, who celebrate its supposed divinity.

Arthur Hughes, *The Knight of the Sun,* oil on board, 1893, private collection, 28 x 40cm (11 x 16in)

This is a smaller version of a painting that was executed in 1860. Hughes painted it for Alice Boyd, William Bell Scott's companion. The image is of a knight, whose coat of arms is a sun motif, being taken to a spot where he can see the setting sun for the last time before he dies. He is seen offering his final prayers as the sun drops below the horizon.

JW Waterhouse, *Ophelia,* oil on canvas, 1894, private collection, 124 x 74cm (49½ x 29½in)

Waterhouse gives the same attention to detail in nature as Millais did in his version of the same subject that was produced over forty years before, suggesting that Ruskin's tenets still had, for some at least, currency at the end of the nineteenth century. This version shows Ophelia at the river's edge contemplating the fate that awaits her. Her unfulfilled love for Hamlet has resulted in her unbalanced mind, and brought forth conflicting feelings of love and hate.

JW Waterhouse, *La Belle Dame Sans Merci,* oil on canvas, 1893, Hessisches Landesmuseum, Darmstadt, Germany, 112 x 81cm (44½ x 32½in)

The Beautiful Lady Without Pity, the English translation of this painting's title, is a poem that was written by John Keats in 1819 and was the inspiration for this picture. The poem reads 'I met a lady in the meads, Full beautiful – a faery's child, Her hair was long, her foot was light, And her eyes were wild'. Several artists of the late Pre-Raphaelite period were similarly inspired by the poem.

E Burne-Jones, *The Angel Gabriel, Part of an Annunciation,* oil on panel, 1893, private collection, 85 x 85cm (34 x 34in)

Burne-Jones had originally painted a version of *The Annunciation* in 1879, which depicted an engagement between the Angel Gabriel and the Virgin Mary. In this version the background is inspired by 15th-century *quattrocento* painting, but the figure is not instantly recognizable as Burne-Jones, with the simplified facial features common to his stained glass designs. It is assumed that this was originally part of a diptych.

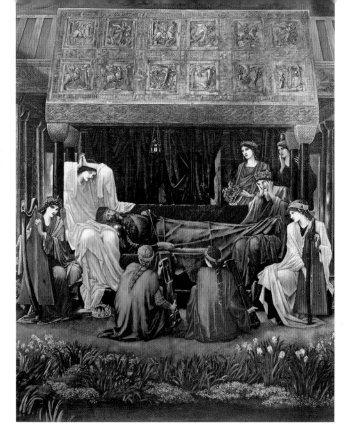

E Burne-Jones, *Last Sleep of Arthur in Avalon*, oil on canvas, 1881–98, Museo de Arte de Ponce, Puerto Rico, 645 x 282cm (258 x 112½in)

This huge painting was the culmination of twenty years work, occupying the artist up until his death in 1898.

Many view it as his masterpiece, due to its scale and attention to detail; Burne-Jones himself described it as 'my chief dream'. The *mise en scene* shows King Arthur dying, overseen by his court, and epitomizes the nexus of his *oeuvre*, the moment between serenity and activity.

WH Hunt, *The Lady of Shalott*, oil on panel, 1886–1905, Manchester Art Gallery, UK, 44 x 34cm (17½ x 13½in)

Hunt first approached this subject in 1857, when he produced a drawing for the Moxon Tennyson. The poet criticized him at the time for over elaborating the figure beyond her description in his text. Three decades later, and despite failing eyesight, he produced this extraordinarily detailed painting, which held back on fantastical elements but contained far more detail and embellishment than the original drawing.

JW Waterhouse, *The Awakening of Adonis*, oil on canvas, 1899, private collection, 96 x 188cm (38½ x 75in)

Percy Shelley wrote *Adonais* as an elegy to his fellow poet John Keats. It is based on the myth of Adonis, who was reborn after Aphrodite poured nectar on his dead body. Each drop of his blood from the wound then turned into an anemone, as Waterhouse has shown.

E Burne-Jones, *The Arming and Departure of the Knights,* tapestry, 1895–6, Birmingham Museum and Art Gallery, UK, 360 x 244cm (144 x 97½in)

This was part of a series of tapestries that were designed by Burne-Jones for Morris & Co. as part of a commission for Compton Hall, near Wolverhampton. This panel depicts the Knights of the Round Table setting off from Camelot in their quest to find the Holy Grail. Much of the detailed heraldry was referenced and designed by William Morris. Queen Guinevere is seen handing Sir Lancelot his shield to the left of the picture.

INDEX

Aesthetic Movement 26, 27, 29, 50, 80, 133, 161, 189, 201, 207, 214, 216, 228, 241
Albert, Prince Consort 6, 65
Arthurian legends 6, 23, 38, 40–1, 119, 159, 171, 185, 203, 243, 247, 252, 253
Arts and Crafts movement 7, 42, 162

Balfour, Arthur 241, 245
Balzac, Honoré de 38
Baudelaire, Charles 16
Bellini, Vincenzo
  I Puritani 119
Blake, William 38
Bloomsbury Group 98–9
Boccaccio, Giovanni 14, 143
Bodley, George Frederick 157
Moxon Tennyson 23, 27, 27, 40, 137, 252
Booth, Charles 72
Botticelli, Sandro 86
  Dante Alighieri 33
Boyce, George
  Annie Miller 63
Brett, John
  The Hedger 152
  The Mountains of St Gingolph 159
Brock, Thomas
  JE Millais 29
Broomfield, Frances
  Rossetti's Menagerie 45
Brown, Emma 78, 78, 129, 188, 209, 220
Brown, Ford Madox 32–3, 43, 49, 50, 64, 70, 76–81, 78, 83, 103, 161, 238
  The Artist's Wife Emma 79
  The Body of Harold Brought BeforeWilliam the Conqueror 163
  The Bromley Children 79
  The Bromley Family 78
  Byron's Dream 216
  children 78, 81
  Convalescent 209
  Cordelia's Portion (1866–72) 211
  Cordelia's Portion (1867–75) 221
  The Corsair's Return 204
  Crabtree Watching the Transit of Venus 247
  Cromwell on his Farm 219
  Cromwell on his Farm at St Ives 135
  The Crucifixion 157
  Dalton Collecting Marsh Fire Gas 249
  Dream of Sardanapalus 81, 206
  I due Foscari 190
  Elijah Restoring the Widow's Son 189
  Emma Madox Brown 188
  An English Autumn Afternoon 123, 131
  The English Boy 148
  The Entombment 80, 81
  The Execution of Mary, Queen of Scots 76, 76
  The Expulsion of the Danes 80
  The Finding of Don Juan by Haidee 190
  The First Translation of the Bible into English... 33, 105
  Geoffrey Chaucer Reading the 'Legend of Custance'...77, 78, 105, 113
  Hampstead 79
  Heath St, Hampstead 130

The Irish Girl 148, 149
Italian Fisher Boy 141
Jacob and Joseph's Coat 208
Jesus Washing Peter's Feet 78, 79, 226
King René's Honeymoon 171
The Last of England 78, 94, 127, 130, 188
Madeline Scott 240
Manchester Murals 81, 240, 247, 249
Manfred on the Jungfrau 154
marriages 78–9, 79
May Memories 220
My Native Land, Goodnight 188
The Nativity 80
The Nosegay 184
Pretty Baa Lambs 74, 78, 79, 142
Romeo and Juliet 183
St Oswald Receiving St Aidan 179
The Seeds and Fruits of English Poetry 77, 77
Self Portrait(1877) 226
Self-portrait (1850) 111
Stages of Cruelty 139
stained glass 80, 157, 162, 179
Tell's Son 232
Waiting: An English Fireside 129
William Michael Rossetti... 132
Windermere 131
Work 79, 130, 148, 153, 175
Bulwer Lytton, Edward 56, 107
Burne-Jones, Edward 41, 42, 50, 75, 82–7, 83, 85, 125, 161, 201, 237
  Alleluia 243
  Angel Gabriel... 251
  Angels Climbing and Descending 85
  Angels of Creation 246
  The Arming and Departure of the Knights 253
  Astrologia 174
  Autumn 193
  The Baleful Head 245
  Beatrice 195
  The Beguiling of Merlin 214, 219
  Briar Rose series 238
  children 83
  The Council Chamber 248
  The Cumaean Sibyl 228
  Cupid and Psyche 84, 172
  Danäe... 244
  Days of Creation 227
  The Doom Fulfilled 241
  The Evening Star 195
  The Failure of Sir Lancelot 247
  Fair Rosamund and Queen Eleanor 156
  The Finding of Medusa 240
  The Flight: St George Kills the Dragon 177
  and Francis Graham 234, 242
  Garden of the Hesperides 213
  The Golden Stairs 86, 233
  Green Summer 185
  The Honeymoon of King René of Anjou 162
  Hymenaeus 186
  King Cophetua and the Beggar Maid 87, 242
  King René's Wedding 196
  Knights and the Briar Rose 192
  The Knight's Farewell 83, 83
  Last Sleep of Arthur in Avalon 252

Laus Veneris 85, 221
The Legend of St Frideswide 144
Lot and his Daughters 216
Love that Moves the Sun 234
The March Marigold 203
and Maria Zambaco 84, 85, 86, 186, 195, 219
marriage 43, 83
The Merciful Knight 168
Merlin and Nimue... 84–5, 159
The Mill 86, 234
The Mirror of Venus 230
Oxford Union murals 41, 82
Pan and Psyche 200
Perseus series 240, 245
Phyllis and Demophoön 85, 199
Portrait of Marie Spartali 238
Princess Sabra Led to the Dragon 176
The Prioress's Tale 82, 83
Pygmalion series 86, 87, 222
The Resurrection 161
The Rock of Doom 237
St Cecilia 173
Sibylla Delphica 186
Sidonia the Sorceress 153
The Sirens 220, 237
The Sleeping Beauty 207
The Soul Attains 222
stained glass 82, 85, 144, 161, 162, 162, 216, 246
Study for the Head of Nimue 214
Study for 'The Sleeping Princess' 238
tapestries 234, 243, 247, 253
The Tree of Forgiveness 239
The Wheel of Fortune 241
William Morris Working... 218
Winter 201
Burne-Jones, Georgiana 75, 83, 87, 185, 195
Burton, William Shakespeare
  The Wounded Cavalier 128
Butterfield, William 72, 193
Byron, Lord 77, 216
  Adieu, Adieu My Native Land 188
  Don Juan 190
  Manfred 154
  Sardanapalus 206
  The Two Foscari 190

Cabanel, Alexandre 182
Caine, Hall 51
Camden Town Group 99
Carlyle, Thomas 29, 60, 78, 79, 82, 175, 221

Chartism 56
Chatterton, Thomas 97, 136
Chaucer, Geoffrey 6, 14, 84, 113
Collins, Charles 19, 90
  Convent Thoughts 90, 91, 112
  The Good Harvest 125
  Wilkie Collins 91
Collins, Wilkie 64, 65, 70, 90, 91
Collinson, James 7, 58, 96
  The Charity Boy's Debut 96, 97
  The Renunciation of the Queen of Hungary 110
Combe, Thomas 18–19, 56, 57, 60, 62, 63, 64, 70, 90, 115, 146
Constable, John 65, 123
Cope, Charles West 98
Cornforth, Fanny 37, 42–3, 42, 45, 51, 143, 145, 155, 159, 171, 185, 196, 230
Coronio, Aglaia 234
Coronio, Calliope 189
Correggio
  Madonna of the Basket 16–17
Cowper, Frank Cadogan 98
  La Belle Dame Sans Merci 98
Crimean War 22, 23, 129, 135, 140

Dalziel brothers
  The Bible Gallery 189
Dante Alighieri 6, 31, 32, 33, 38–9, 83, 121, 146, 182, 192, 194, 195, 205, 217, 222, 232, 233
de Morgan, Evelyn 237
  The Angel of Death 247
Delacroix, Eugène 76
Deverell, Walter 36, 58, 96, 111
  Twelfth Night 36, 96, 108
Dickens, Charles 16, 17, 24, 55, 90, 98, 106, 149, 165
Dodgson, Charles 26, 33, 91, 166
Donizetti, Gaetano
  La fille du regiment 126
Dunn, Henry Treffry 47
  Calliope Coronio, after Rossetti 47
Dyce, William
  King Lear and the Fool in the Storm 115
  The Woman of Samaria 154

Egg, Augustus 68, 70, 111
Exposition Universelle 19, 25

Fairbairn, Thomas 59, 170
Fine Art Society 71, 72–3
Fisk, WH
  Frederic George Stephens 96
Flandrin, Jean Hippolyte 34
  Study for the Resurrection of Christ 34
'Fleshy Scandal' 49
Foord, Tryphena 91, 132
Foster, Miles Birkett 162, 177
Frith, William Powell 98
  Charles Dickens 16
  A Private View at the Royal Academy 27

Gambart, Ernest 26–7, 28, 63, 79
Garrick Club 24, 25, 29
The Germ 15, 16, 36, 78, 90, 94, 132
Gilman, Harold
  A London Street in the Snow 99

Gothic Revival 44, 157, 193
Graham, Frances 234, 242
Graham, William 85, 212, 225, 227, 231
Great Exhibition 7, 64, 82
Greaves, Walter
   Whistler in Cremorne Gardens 46
Grosvenor Gallery 50, *50*, 70, 87, 228, 230, 242

Hogarth, William 7, 65, 249
   Falstaff Examining his Recruits 6
Houses of Parliament murals 77, 163
Hughes, Arthur 90–1, *90*
   The Annunciation 142
   April Love 91, *132*
   The Brave Geraint 91
   Fair Rosamund 120
   The Guarded Bower 176
   Home From the Sea 164
   Home from Work 160
   Jack o'Lantern 211
   The Knight of the Sun 250
   The Lady with the Lilacs 166
   The Long Engagement 91, *144*
   marriage 91, 132
   Musidora Bathing 90
   Ophelia 90–1, *114*
   Oxford Union murals 41, 91
   The Pained Heart 187
   Sir Galahad: Quest of the Holy Grail 203
Hunt, Cyril Benoni 66, *67*, 68, 69, 70, 71
Hunt, Emily 62, 156
Hunt, William Holman 19, *19*, 32, 33, 34, 52–73, 55, 57, 61, *73*, 161
   The Afterglow in Egypt 60, 61, *166*
   Amaryllis 242
   Annie Miller 58
   and Annie Miller 59, 62, 64
   Arab Resting by a Stream 60
   Asparagus Island 147
   The Awakening Conscience 37, 59
   Bianca 67, *191*
   Cairo: Sunset on the Gebel Makattum 122
   children 66, 67, 68, 69, 70–1, *70*, 71
   Christ Among the Doctors 61, 245
   Christ and the Two Marys 55, *104*
   Claudio and Isabella 111
   A Converted British Family... 36, 57, 112
   Courtyard of a House in Damietta... 65
   Distant View of Nazareth 66
   Edward Lear 138
   Fairlight Downs... 133
   Fanny Holman Hunt 64
   The Festival of St Swithuns 62
   The Finding of the Saviour in the Temple 63, *163*, 245
   The Flight of Madeline and Porphyro... (The Eve of St Agnes) 53, 55, 57,
   Hanna Hadoub affair 61
   Hercules in the Garden of the Hesperides 244
   The Hireling Shepherd 38, 59, 60, 98, *114*
   Holy Land 52, 60–1, 62, 64–9, 71, 122, 123, 125, 128, 130, 163, 166, 225, 249
   Honest Labour has a Comely Face 156
   The Importunate Neighbour 72
   Isabella and the Pot of Basil 180
   The Lady of Shalott 63, *109*, 244, 252

The Lanternmaker's Courtship 150
The Light of the World 59, *59*, 60, 71, 72–3, *118*
Little Nell and her Grandfather 55, *55*
London Bridge on...the Marriage of the Prince...of Wales 66
Love at First Sight 56, 57
marriages 62, 64, 66, 69–70, 72, 73, 94
Master Hilary – the Tracer 70, *71*
May Morning on Magdalen College Tower 70, 71
The Miracle of the Sacred Fire 71, 249
Miss Flamborough 235
Moxon Tennyson 63, *63*, 252
Mrs Fairbairn and her Children 59, *170*
Mrs Sarah Wilson 69
My Son Cyril 71
Il Dolce far Niente 179
Old Church Ewell 54
Our English Coasts (Strayed Sheep) 116
The Plain of Esdraelon... 70
Plain of Rephaim 130
Ponte Vecchio, Florence 67
Rienzi... 56, 57, *107*
Robert Braithwaite Martineau 65, *135*
The Scapegoat 60, 62–3, *128*
The Schoolgirl's Hymn 146
Self-portrait 52, *61*
The Shadow of Death 68, *213*
The Sphinx, Giza... 123
Study of a Bloodhound 54
Study for the Head of Valentine 71
Talking-whispering in the Synagogue 225
Triumph of the Innocents 69, 71, 225
Valentine Rescuing Sylvia from Proteus 58, *58*, *103*
The Walls of Jerusalem 68

Inchbold, John William
   The White Doe of Rylstone (From Bolton) 127
Ingres, Jean Auguste Dominique 149, 182
International Exhibition 64–5
Ionides, Alexander 85, 189

Japonisme 47, 172, 201, 216

Keats, John 6, 77, 151, 252
   La Belle Dame Sans Merci 251
   The Eve of St Agnes 55, 106
   Isabella 14, 109, 180
Kelmscott Manor 48, *48*, 49, 50, 93, 204, 209, 215, 218

Leathart, James 79, 81

Legros, Alphonse
   William Michael Rossetti 33
Leighton, Frederic 29, 63, 98, 201
   Cimabue's Madonna 24
Leyland, Frederick 80, 85, 178, 180, 185, 211, 216, 219, 229, 230

Maclise, Daniel 77
   Henry Sass 13
Malory, Sir Thomas
   Le Morte d'Arthur 40–1, 119, 159, 171, 185, 247
Manet, Édouard 44
   Le Déjeuner sur l'herbe 45
   Olympia 45, *45*
Martineau, Robert Braithwaite 65, 135, *135*, 138
   A Girl with a Cat 153
   The Last Day in the Old Home 135
Masaccio, Tommaso
   Madonna Casini 35
Memling, Hans
   Triptych 35
Michelangelo 86, 241
Millais, John Everett 9, 11–29, *11*, *29*, 55, 66, 90, 98, 125
   Accepted 22
   An Actor 23
   Alfred Lord Tennyson 23
   Alice Gray 136
   Apple Blossoms – Spring 136, 143
   Autumn Leaves 25, 28, *133*, 136, 143
   The Black Brunswicker 26, 28, *28*, *149*, *181*
   The Blind Girl 22, 26, *134*
   The Boyhood of Raleigh 27
   The Bridesmaid 111
   Bubbles 29
   Cherry Ripe 28, 29
   children 26, *26*, 27, 28
   Christ in the Carpenter's Shop 16–17, *106*
   The Death of Romeo and Juliet 104
   Drawing from the antique 13
   A Dream of the Past – Sir Isumbras 28, 94, *137*, 154
   Effie Ruskin 25
   L'Enfant du Regiment 126
   The Escape of a Heretic 138
   Esther 29
   The Eve of St Agnes 27, 29
   Ferdinand Lured by Ariel 97, *108*
   Glenfinlas with Millais Fishing 21
   Hark 55
   Head of Mariana 16
   Holman Hunt 19
   A Huguenot on St Bartholomew's Day... 19, 20, 22, *26*, 26, 116
   Isabella 14–15, 17, 56, *109*
   James Wyatt and his Granddaughter 14
   John Ruskin 20–1, *20*, 22
   A Knight Errant 197
   Lorenzo and Isabella 14–15, *15*, 17
   Mariana 113
   marriage 11, 20–1, 22, 24–5, 26, *26*, 27, 38, 121
   Moxon Tennyson 23, 27, *27*
   My First Sermon 29, *165*
   News from Home 140
   Ophelia 18, 19, 25, 36, 90–1, *117*, 149, *168*
   The Order of Release 10, 20, 25, 64, *118*, 119
   The Parable of the Tares 29

Peace Concluded 22, *135*
Pizarro Seizing the Inca of Peru 13, *13*
Portrait a Girl 29
Portrait Head of Rossetti 30
The Proscribed Royalist 22, *119*
The Rescue 24, 26, *124*
The Return of the Dove to the Ark 25, 90, *102*
St Martin's Summer 143
Self-portrait (1847) 13, *15*
Self-portrait 21
Sir Henry Irving 29
Sisters 27
The Somnambulist 29
The Sound of Many Waters 223
A Souvenir of Velasquez 29
Study of Effie Gray 23
Study for the Head of Ferdinand 15
Thomas Carlyle 29
Thomas Combe 56
The Tribe of Benjamin Seizing the Daughters of Shiloh 13
Turner on Varnishing Day 21
The Vale of Rest 28, 143
Waiting 121
The Waterfall at Glenfinlas 120
A Wife 24
William Gladstone 29
Winter Fuel 143
The Woodman's Daughter 17, *115*
Miller, Annie 58, 59, 62, 63, 64, 179, 205
Morris, Jane 42, *42*, 46, 49, 50, 75, 190, 194, 195, *195*, 198, 199, 202, 205, 209, 215, 230, 232, 239
Morris, Jenny 75, 93, *204*, 215
Morris, Marshall, Faulkner & Co./Morris and Co. 44, 46, 48, 84, 93
Morris, May 75, 93, 202, 205, *205*, 210, *210*, 212, 215, 222
Morris, William 7, 39, 41, 44, 75, 82, 84, 93, *93*, 95, 125, 132, 146, 253
   Iceland 93, 204
   Kelmscott Press 48, 83, 84, 243
   Lapse of the Year 193
   marriage 42, 46, 48, 93
   as model 49, 159
   News from Nowhere 48
   Oxford Union murals 41, 93
   poetry 93, 241
   political beliefs 86–7, 93
   textiles 210, 218

Old Watercolour Society 85, 86
Overbeck, Friedrich 76
   The Adoration of the Kings 76
Oxford Movement 7, 41, 60, 82, 90, 93, 106, 157, 162
Oxford Union murals 40, 41, 82, 91, 93, 139

plein air painting 56, 79, 108, 130, 142
Plint, Thomas 17, 148, 175
Post-Impressionism 98, 99
Poynter, Edward
   Georgiana Burne-Jones 87
Pre-Raphaelitism journal 19
Prinsep, Val 63
   Woman Reclining with a Parrot 62
Pugin, Augustus Welby Northmore 7, 105

Raphael 6
   The Transfiguration 7, 56
Reynolds, Sir Joshua 6, 12–13, 34, 65, 165

Self-portrait 6
Richmond, William Blake 72
  Florence Nightingale 73
Rooke, Thomas 86
  *Interior of the Home of Edward
    Burne-Jones* 86
Rossetti, Christina 32, *32, 33,* 34, 91,
    95, 96, 176, 193
Rossetti, Dante Gabriel 7, 9, 30–51, *30,
    33, 39, 51,* 58–9, 70, 76, 82, 83,
    93, 125, 161, 201
  Angel Offering a Censer 157
  and Annie Miller 62
  The Annunciation (1855) 38
  The Annunciation (1861–2) 162
  Arthur's Tomb 38, 40, *119*
  Aspecta Medusa 178
  Astarte Syriaca 49, 50–1, 227
  Beata Beatrix 36, 43, 46, *192*
  *Beatrice Meeting Dante at a Marriage
    Feast…* 31
  La Bella Mano 222
  The Beloved 45, *172*
  Blanzifiore 215
  The Blessed Damozel 45, 51, 225, 231
  The Blue Bower 171
  The Blue Closet 137
  Bocca Baciata 143
  The Borgia Family 107, *167*
  The Bower Meadow 49, 202, 208
  Bruna Brunelleschi 230
  Calliope Coronio 47, 189
  Christ Preaching 193
  Christina Rossetti 32, 176
  collections 45, *45,* 46, 47, 50
  Dante in Meditation 39
  Dante's Dream 39, 205, 217
  Dantis Amor 39, 146
  Death of Lady Macbeth 223
  La Donna della Fiamma 198
  La Donna della Finestra 232
  Ecce Ancilla Domini! 35, 105
  and Elizabeth Siddal 36, 38–9,
    40–3
  Elizabeth Siddal (1854) 122
  Elizabeth Siddal (1855) 37
  Elizabeth Siddal (c.1860) 43
  Elizabeth Siddal Reading 37
  Fair Rosamund 42, 155
  Fanny Cornforth 42
  Fazio's Mistress 42
  *The First Anniversary of the Death of
    Beatrice* 36, 38, 41, 82, 121
  'Fleshy Scandal' 49
  Found 37, 145
  Frederick Leyland 230
  La Ghirlandata 212
  The Girlhood of Mary Virgin 33,
    34, *34*
  Glorious Gwendolen's golden hair 41
  Hand and Soul 36
  Hanging the Mistletoe 149
  Head of a woman called Ruth 51
  Helen of Troy 165
  Hesterna Rosa 174
  *The Honeymoon of King René of
    Anjou* 162
  How They Met Themselves 43, *150*
  illness 46–7, 48, 49, 50–1
  and Jane Morris 41, 42, 46–7, 48–9,
    50, 185, 190, 194, 195, 198,
    199, 215, 230, 232
  Jane Morris (1857) 42
  Jane Morris (1861) 47
  Jane Morris (1870) 195
  Jenny Morris Aged 10 204

  Joan of Arc… 164
  Joli Coeur 181
  King René's Honeymoon 147
  Lady Lilith 8–9, 185
  The Lady of Pity 194
  The Lady of Shalott 100–1
  Ligeia Siren 212
  The Loving Cup 180, 202
  Marigolds 218
  marriage 36, 41, 43, 150,
    151, 192
  Mary at the House of St John 140
  Mary Magdalene 228
  Mary Magdalene at the Door…
    43, 145
  May Morris 210
  May Morris Aged 9 205
  menagerie 45, *45,* 47
  Mnemosyne 235
  Moxon Tennyson 40, 137
  Mrs William Morris 185
  My Lady Greensleeves 167
  The One Hope 48
  Oxford Union murals 40, 41, 139
  Pandora (1869) 190
  Pandora (1871) 207
  Paolo and Francesca da Rimini 182
  poetry 32, 36, 43, 46, 48–9, 49, 50,
    51, 185, 196, 206, 222, 238
  The Portrait 185
  Portrait of a Lady 198
  Portrait of Swinburne 44
  Proserpina 206
  Proserpine 49, 239
  The Quest of the Holy Grail 40
  Il Ramoscello 173
  Regina Cordium (1860) 151
  Regina Cordium (1866) 151
  Robert Browning 126
  A Roman Widow 216
  *Rossetti Being Sketched by Elizabeth
    Siddal* 117
  The Salutation of Beatrice 233
  The Salutation of Beatrice in Eden
    38–9, 38
  A Sea Spell 229
  Self-portrait (1849) 35
  Self-portrait (1855) 129
  The Sermon on the Mount 159
  Sibylla Palifera 197
  Silence 199
  Sir Galahad at the Ruined Chapel 41
  *Sir Lancelot in the Queen's
    Bedchamber* 40
  Sir Lancelot's Vision 139
  stained glass 44, 157, 159, 162, *162,*
    169, 193
  Stillborn Love 48
  Study for David 49

Study of a Female Nude 202
Study for the Figure of Love 217
Study of Mrs William Morris 215
*Study for 'The Blessed
  Damozel'* 225
Study for 'The Bower Meadow' 202
*To Caper Nimbly in a Lady's
  Chamber…* 107
Venus Verticordia (1864–8) 187
Venus Verticordia (1867) 182
Veronica Veronese 211
The Visitation 44
Water Willow 209
The Wedding of St George 169
Woman with a Fan 196
Rossetti, Maria 32, 33
Rossetti, William Michael 6, 20, 32, 33,
    34, 38, 45, 49, 51, 56, 64, 78, 95,
    121, 132, *132*
Ruskin, Effie 19, 20–1, 23, 25, 62,
    92, 118
Ruskin, John 6, 7, 7, 11, 14, 18, *19,*
    20–1, *20,* 22, 36, 38, 39, 55, 57,
    60, 67, 71, 79, 82, 83, 84–5, 92,
    93, 117, 120, 127, 129, *95,*
    141, 161
  Gweiss Rock at Glenfinlas 92
  Modern Painters 6, 19, 55, 56, 92,
    104, 137
  'pathetic fallacy' 28, 137, 187
  Pre-Raphaelitism 19, 92
  The Seven Lamps of Architecture 18, 92
  The Stones of Venice 18, 84, 92
  Whistler vs Ruskin 87

Sandys, Frederick 94
  Autumn 154
  Loves Shadow 183
  Mary Magdalene 94, 152
  *Morgan Le Fay: Queen of
    Avalon* 171
  A Nightmare 94
  The Old Chartist 56
  Perdita 178
  Self-portrait 94
Sass, Henry 12, *13,* 32, 96
Scott, Sir Walter 32, 55, 131
Scott, William Bell 7, 39, 46, 47, 50, 68,
    70, 95, 108
  Algernon Charles Swinburne 140
  John Ruskin… 95
  King Egfrid 158
  poetry 95
  The Trial of William Wallace 131
  Una and the Lion 151
  Wallington Hall murals 95, 158
Seddon, Thomas 60, 68
Shakespeare, William 6, *18,* 19, 23, 58,
    67, 77, 94, 96, 107, 108, 111,
    113, 114, 115, 117, 168, 178,
    183, 187, 211, 221, 223, 250
Shelley, Percy Bysshe
  Adonais 252
Shields, Frederick
  The Dead Rossetti 51
Sickert, Walter 98, 99
Siddal, Elizabeth 18, 36–7, 37, 38–9,
    40–3, 43, 58, 96, 108, 117, 121,
    122, 151, 159
Solomon, Simeon 95
  The Painter's Pleasurance 95
  Night 224
  Shadrach, Meshac and Abednego 169
  A vision of love revealed in sleep 224
Spartali, Marie 205, 208, 234, 238
  Spencer, Edmund

The Faerie Queen 151
Stanhope, John Roddam Spencer 247
  Eve Tempted 229
  The Labours of Psyche 214
Stephen, Leslie 64, 72
Stephens, Frederic George 6, 62, 69,
    70, 96, 97, 133, 174
Swinburne, Algernon 44, 49, 64, 95,
    140, 226
  Laus Veneris 221
  Symbolist Movement 105, 109, 224

Tennyson, Alfred Lord 23, *23,* 25, 40,
    64, 95, 133, 151
  The Day-Dream 238
  The Lady of Shalott 23, 101, 109,
    243, 252
  Mariana 16, 23, 113
  The Miller's Daughter 91, 132
  Moxon edition 23, 27, *27,* 40, 63,
    137, 252
'truth to materials' 18, 92
'truth to nature' 20, 56, 59, 60, 90,
    98, 161
Turner, JMW 6, 18, 19, 20, *21,* 92,
    98, 159

van Eyck, Jan 34, 86
Verdi, Giuseppe
  I due Foscari 190
Victoria, Queen 6, 17, *17,* 65, 68

Wallis, Henry 97
  Chatterton 97, 136, 159
  The Stonebreaker 97, *97*
Waterhouse, John William 237
  The Awakening of Adonis 252
  La Belle Dame Sans Merci 251
  Circe Offering the Cup to Ulysses 248
  The Lady of Shalott 243
  Ophelia 250
Watts, George Frederick 189, 201
  Edward Burne-Jones 85
  Thomas Carlyle 77
Watts-Dunton, Theodore 51, 226
Waugh, Edith 66–7, 68, 69–70, 69, 72,
    73, 94
Waugh, Evelyn 47, 229
Waugh, Fanny 64–6, *64,* 67, 68,
    94, 179
Webb, Philip 39, 42, 44, *83,* 93, 162
Whistler, James McNeill 29, 44, *46,* 47,
    50, 94, 98, 189, 201
  Peacock Room 80, 216
  *Symphony in White, No. 1: The White
    Girl* 29, 45
  *Thames: Nocturne in Blue and
    Silver* 99
  Whistler vs Ruskin 87
White, David Thomas 26
Wilde, Oscar 219
Wilding, Alexa 45, 175, 178, 182, 185,
    187, 197, 205, 208, 211, 212,
    222, 225, 229
Winterhalter, Franz Xaver
  Queen Victoria 17
Woolner, Thomas 7, 64, 66, 67, 90, 94,
    127, 139
  Tennyson 95
Wordsworth, William 77, 151
  The White Doe of Rylstone 127
Working Men's College 38, 83
Wyatt, James 14, 15

Zambaco, Maria *84,* 85, 186, 195, 198,
    219, 234